WAYNESBURG COLLEGE LIBRARY
WAYNESBURG, PA.

S0-BSZ-169

861   G9582p
Guillen, Nicolas
Patria o Muerte
101935

¡PATRIA O MUERTE!
The Great Zoo
and other poems

¡PATRIA O MUERTE!
The Great Zoo
and other poems
by Nicolás Guillén

**Translated and edited
by Robert Márquez**

**Monthly Review Press
New York and London**

Copyright © 1972 by Robert Márquez
All Rights Reserved

Library of Congress Catalog Card Number: 72–81758

First Printing

Monthly Review Press
116 West 14th Street, New York, N.Y. 10011
33/37 Moreland Street, London, E.C. 1

Manufactured in the United States of America

For Madelaine,
with love,
in fulfillment of a promise
and
for my family,
with love,
in partial fulfillment
of a hope.
   —Robert Márquez

101935

Indice

Contents

Introduction

Other Poems: 1925–1969

Introduction

Despite the current vogue among publishers for all forms of neo-African literature and a complimentary flowering of interest in writers from the Third World, Nicolás Guillén's name is still generally unfamiliar to the American reading public. This is unfortunate, for along with Pablo Neruda, César Vallejo, and García Lorca, all already widely translated, Guillén, poet laureate of revolutionary Cuba, represents the very best in Hispanic poetry and is at the same time the undisputed leader of an important trend in contemporary Latin American letters. Guillén is also an open stylist whose manner does not simply anticipate a coterie audience. The publication of this anthology-translation is therefore timely and particularly satisfying.

Since his first widely acclaimed *Motivos de son* (1930), Guillén, a mulatto, has been regarded as the major exponent of Black poetry in the Spanish-speaking world. But his thematic scope is wide, and although primarily known as a poet of folk rhythms, Black and popular themes, he is also recognized for his humor, for his artistic refinement, for the sensitivity of his love ballads, and for the compassionate poignancy of his political and revolutionary verse. He is not, strictly speaking, a poet of Negritude. Unlike Aimé Césaire and the poets of the French and English Caribbean, his concern with Negro culture and his condemnation of white hypocrisy and injustice do not include a direct repudiation of European (in this case Spanish) cultural traditions. Guillén is more properly the poet of a

---

A Spanish version of this introduction appeared in the Cuban journal *Casa de las Américas*, (marzo-junio, 1971), translated by Armando Álvarez Bravo.

people and his principle concern has been the creation of a poetry with a distinctively Cuban flavor, one which reflects—and helps consolidate—the Cuban national identity. It is as a Cuban that he (like Frantz Fanon) envisages the wretched of the earth as victims of a common oppression, and it is in this sense that, as the great Argentine critic and thinker Ezequiel Martínez Estrada has observed, "All his work is a battle against oppression, against the privileges and rivalries that separate human beings of whatever condition."

Guillén was born in 1902 in the provincial town of Camagüey. He received his earliest education in the local Catholic and public schools, but until the age of fifteen it was the influence of his father that was decisive. The elder Guillén, a silversmith turned newspaper editor, first introduced him to the lure of printer's ink and to what was to become his second great professional preoccupation, journalism. In the family library, under his father's tutelage, the young Guillén was first exposed to the Spanish classics. His father, a veteran of the Cuban War for Independence, was also an active member of the provincial Partido Liberal leadership and, besides helping with the small chores involved in the publication of the newspaper *Las dos repúblicas*—and, later, *La Libertad*—Guillén was permitted to sit in during discussions of national political issues. Thus the elder Guillén served as the child's literary and political mentor. The death of his father in 1917, at the hands of conservative government troops, was a severe blow. It meant, as Guillén's biographer Ángel Augier points out, "the loss of his friend and teacher, of his firmest spiritual support." *

---

* Augier's two-volume biography, *Nicolás Guillén: Notas para un estudio biográfico-crítico* (Santa Clara: Universidad de Las Villas,

14

The death of Guillén's father was followed by a period of economic hardship and bohemian indecisiveness. He assumed responsibility for the family fortunes and, with his brother Francisco, went to work as a typesetter for a local printer. Eventually he spent a year studying law at the University of Havana, but, disappointed with the general atmosphere in the capital, he dropped his studies and returned to Camagüey. It was during this period of uncertainty that Guillén began to show the signs of his poetic gift. His first poems appeared in the early 1920's in *Camagüey gráfico*, a local journal of arts and letters, and bore the stamp of the Modernist influence. Modernism had reached its apogee and, with the death of Rubén Darío in 1916, had begun its decline throughout most of Latin America. In Cuba, however, where that exuberant fascination with the exquisite and with formal perfection had had its own precursors in the work of José Martí and Julián del Casal, the movement lingered and for a time competed with the emerging esthetic of *Los nuevos* (The New Ones). Thus Guillén, like the majority of the writers of his generation, began his poetic career in the shadow of Rubén Darío. But it was "the worst Darío," he later confessed, "the Darío of tintypes and enamels, with swans, fountains, abbots, pages, counts, marchionesses, and all those other knick-knacks." He founded and edited *Lis*, a literary magazine with a Modernist allegiance, and by 1922 had managed to complete his first small book of poems, a collection whose rather unpoetic title, *Cerebro y corazón*

1964–1965), is the only work of its kind available on Guillén. It is an excellent work that spans the years 1902 to 1948, and anyone interested in the poet will owe it a special debt. I am particularly indebted to Augier for the exhaustiveness of his biographical data.

(Head and Heart), hinted at the author's tragic ambivalence. It was a derivative work of little poetic distinction which, to the writer's credit, he never published,* but which does give us some sense of Guillén's developing technical and rhythmic expertise and of his skeptical and misanthropic outlook at the time. "Lord, Lord, . . . why is humanity so evil?" he pleads in a tone reminiscent of the decadent poets. *Cerebro y corazón* also evinced a tendency to evade reality, an avoidance of the mundane and the popular, and a conception of art that is aristocratic and romantically formalistic.

This collection was followed by a five-year period of silence during which Guillén wrote virtually no poetry but lived immersed in the day-to-day routine of writing articles for newspapers and magazines. His reaction to the literary iconoclasm of the *vanguardistas*—dadaists, surrealists, futurists—appears to have been ambiguous, and although certain of his poems, such as "The Airplane" (written in about 1928), might seem vaguely reminiscent of the futurists, he was to remain on the periphery of their revolt.

With the publication of the *Black Decameron* (1914), Leo Frobenius had laid the foundation for the cult of the primitive; focusing on the folklore and culture of the Negro, it took hold of literature and the arts in Europe after the debacle of the First World War. This new attraction to the world of the Black man was part of the antirationalist and neoromantic response of the intellectuals to the moral collapse of those years. The African and New World Negro, even if not yet accepted as an equal, was everywhere admired for the uninhibited genuineness

---

* It did not become public until very recently, when it appeared as an appendix to the first volume of Augier's biography.

of his reactions to reality, and his art and culture won great popularity as a palliative for the inauthenticity of an exhausted civilization. Jazz was heard in the best salons on the continent. To paraphrase Guillén himself: the Negro reigned while boulevards applauded. This new interest in Black culture and the aesthetic possibilities it presented came to fruition in Blaise Cendrars' *Black Anthology*, in the short stories and commentaries of Paul Morand, in André Gide's *Travels in the Congo*, and in the work of Pablo Picasso and other artists.

This novel fashion in the arts did not reach Spanish America until about 1926 and was, with very few exceptions, limited in its influence to the poets of the Caribbean. It was the Puerto Rican poet Luis Palés Matos who, in his poem "Danza negra," introduced the new motif and the features of style and content that were to characterize its use before—and for some time after—the appearance of Guillén's work.* José Zacarías Tallet and Ramón Guirão, the initiators of the *negrista* movement in Cuba, did not substantially differ with Palés Matos in their treatment of the Black theme. These poets, all of whom were white, regarded the world of the Negro from the vantage point of the outside observer and their poetry, a highly descriptive poetry, depicted him as a picturesque figure who lives primarily through his senses. He "invariably appear[ed] in an atmosphere of violence, heavy sensuality, frenetic dancing and drumming and voodooesque possession. In the case of the female dancers, the most animal and sensuous aspects of her appearance and movements

---

* In Cuba, the scholarly research of Fernando Ortiz into the island's Black heritage lent anthropological depth and intellectual legitimacy to the new movement.

17

are emphasized." * It was a poetry rich in local color and in erotic and musical effects that depended heavily on rhythmic inventiveness and onomatopoeia, but whose detachment from the scenes it presented indicated that these writers were consciously slumming.

When Guillén's next book, *Motivos de son*, appeared, it therefore heralded the appearance of a new authenticity and was an immediate and scandalous success. These eight poetic monologues for the first time allowed the Negro to speak for himself and from his own perspective. They were at the same time based on the repetitive rhythms of the *son*,† were therefore deeply rooted in the Cuban folk tradition, and spotlighted the daily world of the Black *habanero*. In the prologue to the book, Guillén made it clear that unlike those who came before, he intended to

> incorporate into Cuban literature—not simply as a musical motif but rather as an element of true poetry—what might be called the poem-*son* . . . My *sones* can be put to music. but that does not mean they were written precisely for that purpose, but rather with the aim of presenting, in what is perhaps the most appropriate form, representative scenes created with two brush strokes . . . ordinary people just as they move around us. Just as they speak, just as they think.

Nevertheless, Guillén's first published book of poems was not entirely unrelated to the work of his predecessors in the *negrista* movement. The total effect of the collection is comic and picturesque. The poet's vision of the

---

* G. R. Coulthard, *Race and Colour in Caribbean Literature* (London: Oxford University Press, 1962), p. 94.

† A popular Cuban dance, a cross between the blues and the bugaloo.

world of his creations is a mixture of roguishness and sympathetic amusement. He also focuses on the sensual and frivolous features of that world, and though he faithfully transmits the nuances and subtleties of popular Black speech, he highlights the entertaining characteristics of its linguistic distortions of the normative language. Yet the book contains an implicit, compassionate, critique of life in Havana's Black slums—a social dimension almost entirely lacking in the earlier *negrista* poetry. The purists considered the book an affront, but their opposition to it—which was not entirely literary—was dismissed and Guillén's reputation as a poet became firmly established.

A year later (1931) he reissued *Motivos de son*, along with a series of eight new poems, under the title *Sóngoro cosongo*. The new poems did not abandon the sensual accents of the earlier work (e.g., "Madrigal" and "The New Woman") but indicated something of a shift in emphasis and perspective. Guillén dropped the comic distortions of speech which gave the first poems their distinctive flavor in favor of a more normative poetic language that relied on onomatopoeia and *jitanjáforas**** to suggest the totemic and rhythmic world of Africa in Cuba, in combination with the *romance* and other meters more typical of the classical Spanish literary tradition. This gave the poet a new freedom, a broader poetic scope, and with it appear the first insinuations of a poetry of social protest. In "Sugarcane," for example, the reader is given a terse glimpse of the anti-imperialist feelings which are to become one of

* *Jitanjáfora* is a word of no particular meaning invented by the artist and used for its suggestiveness. *Sóngoro cosongo*, for example, is a *jitanjáfora* intended to evoke the mysterious world of Africa and the tomtom.

19

the major preoccupations of Guillén's later poetry.* The Negro, moreover, had ceased to be a superficial personality out of popular folklore and had become a character of some depth, part of the national dilemma, an indispensable part of the national heritage. Guillén was moving toward a clearer definition of his role as the poet of a people. He became concerned with the elaboration of a genuinely Cuban poetry, a poetry which would reflect the true history and racial composition of the island. "These are mulatto verses," he explains in the prologue to the book:

> They share the same elements that enter into the ethnic composition of Cuba . . . the injection of Africa into this country is so deep, and so many capillary currents cross and interweave in our well-irrigated social hydrography, that to decipher the hieroglyphic would be a job for miniaturists.

---

* The degree to which Guillén (already disturbed by the Negro's plight in a racist society) had begun to respond to Cuba's neocolonial dependence on the United States is evident in a letter he wrote to Arthur Schomburg on October 27, 1932. In addition to showing the poet's deepening anguish, the letter reveals his moral strength. It reads in part: "I confess myself deeply pained by the state my country is in, a slave to foreign gold. We live with the water up to our necks, mediatized by the harshest and most peremptory demands. This leads to a cultural stagnation which makes the development of the spirit very difficult. Perhaps, as in Dante's verse, this is the time to say: 'Lasciate ogni speranza.' And in the background of this sombre, tragic, portrait there is the situation of the Negro, running from one side to the other, without direction, the victim of himself and of his white 'brother,' who is worse than Cain, because he is a hypocrite. Still, I don't lose hope. I think that in strong temperaments the difficulties merely redouble the energy, for certain spirits have unknown reserves which surface in every shipwreck. Men are often measured by the magnitude of the conflicts they must confront." (See "Nicolás Guillén Scrapbook," in the New York Public Library, Schomburg Collection.)

Consequently, I think that among us a creole poetry that neglects the Negro would not be truly creole . . . The Negro—in my view—contributes vital essences to our cocktail. And the two races that emerge on the surface on the island, though apparently distant, are linked subterraneously to each other, like those underwater bridges which secretly join two continents. Therefore the spirit of Cuba is *mestizo.* And from the spirit through the skin our true color will emerge.

Guillén's merging of African drums with traditional forms in dealing with the Black theme is a reflection, in the realm of technique, of his search for this *mestizo* spirit.

The publication of *West Indies, Ltd.* (1934), immediately after the revolution which deposed the dictatorship of Machado (1925–1933), marks a significant transition in the development of Guillén's poetry. *Motivos de son* exposed the reader to the anecdotal and purely external; *Sóngoro cosongo* penetrated deeper into the world of the Black but spoke to the whole Cuban nation. With *West Indies, Ltd.*, the poet expands his area of concern to encompass the entire Antillean archipelago. Furthermore, here the elements of social protest come into prominence. The drums and suggestive modes of his previous verse are still evident in "Sensemayá," and there is still, as there will continue to be, the interest in the "mulatto poem." But these strikingly lyrical poems are clear indictments against the abuses and injustices to which the people of the Antilles—and particularly Cubans and Blacks—are collectively subjected under imperialism. The tone is anguished and bitterly elegiac and the mood, though somber, mirrors the frustrations of the incipient revolutionary (see particularly "Riddles" and "Guadeloupe, W.I."). It is the first important step in Guillén's evolution toward Marxism and toward an art of unambiguously militant convictions, although at this stage his protest is a purely visceral indignation, rooted in broadly nationalist and humanitarian ideals with little specific ideological content. "Sabás," however, does offer some indication of the direction in which his thinking will go and of the militancy which will become characteristic of Guillén's verse after 1934.

In 1936 the Spanish Civil War broke out. A year later Guillén, like artists from all over the world sympathetic to the Republican cause, traveled to Spain as one of the Cuban delegates to the antifascist Second International Congress of Writers for the Defense of Culture. In that same year, 1937, he joined the Communist Party and, under the impact of the war, wrote *España, poema en cuatro angustias y una esperanza* (Spain: A Poem in Four Anguishes and a Hope), a poem of epic proportions in which—as in works on the same theme by César Vallejo and Pablo Neruda—the poet laments the Spanish tragedy. He also published his *Cantos para soldados y sones para turistas* (Songs for Soldiers and *Sones* for Tourists), poems in which the *son*, once limited to the realm of the anecdote and the dance, is turned into an instrument for mocking the American tourist in prerevolutionary Cuba and for denouncing the more salient features of American colonialism on the island. The various *cantos* see the soldier—Cuban or European—as a pawn in the service of imperialism whose role will qualitatively change only with a change in the social structure. The tone of these poems is solemn and accusatory and it is clear that Guillén's allegiance is to the great mass of Cuba's dispossessed—although he also shows a genuine compassion for those victims who, like his soldiers, are unaware of the reality of their own situations. This is as clear in "Why, Soldier, does it seem to you . . ." as his anti-fascism is in "Soldiers in Abyssinia."

Guillén spent the next few years traveling in Europe and on a lecture tour of Latin America, acting at the same time as a correspondent for a number of Cuban publications.* His next book of poetry, *El son entero* (The Entire *Son*), which did not appear until 1947, brought together the different elements of theme and style which had by now become representative of the poet's work: the *son*, the "mulatto poem," the atmosphere of pain and accusation. There was also the strict identification with the Negro, wherever he might be, although, as in "Sweat and the Lash," the author had progressed far beyond an interest in the merely picturesque literary motif: "I deny the art that sees in the Negro only a colorful motif and not an intensely human theme," he explained during one of his lectures in 1947. He did not want his readers to forget that, particularly in the United States, the Negro was still being denied his most elemental human rights. He wanted his poems to transmit that reality and, to the degree that it was possible, to incite his public to change it. "I believe," he said in that same lecture, "that the true artist, who is always profoundly human, ought to dedicate himself to the definitive work, the one that is created with the blood and the bones of men."

El son entero was followed in 1958 by *La paloma de vuelo popular* (The Dove of Popular Flight) and *Elegías* (Elegies), in which the melancholic undertones of his previous books and the already implicit identification of

---

* A selection of Guillén's articles written between 1938 and 1962, *Prosa de prisa* (Hasty Prose), was published by the Universidad de las Villas in 1962. A second edition was published in 1963 by Editorial Hernández in Buenos Aires.

Cuba with the rest of Latin America were crystallized. These two books (usually published together) also provide the reader with the substance of Guillén's hopes for the future and with his vision of the revolution as the only real possibility for Cuba's—and by extension, Latin America's—liberation. These are simple songs

> of death and life
> with which to greet a future drenched in blood,
> red as the sheets, as the thighs,
> as the bed
> of a woman who's just given birth.

Implicit in Guillén's concept of a "mulatto poetry" was the universalist premise that, after 1934, had led him to see the Negro as part of the great mass of the disinherited. It was now quite evident that for Guillén—as for Frantz Fanon—the "Negro problem" was not a question of Black men living among whites, but of Black men systematically oppressed by a society that was racist, colonialist, and capitalist, but only accidentally white.

In an effort to combat that society—a society symbolized by the international and domestic policies of the United States—more successfully, Guillén began to employ a number of techniques which, although foreshadowed in his earlier poetry, were used with increasing frequency in his later books. He began, for example, to sprinkle his verse with words and phrases from standard American English with an intent that recalls the hidden meanings behind the title of *West Indies, Ltd.* Many of these poems are addressed directly to the racial and political situation in the United States as well as other parts of the world (see "Puerto Rican Song"), and, as a result, figures from contemporary politics begin to make their appearance. The specificity with which Guillén indicts individuals like Eisenhower, Nixon, Orville Faubus, and a host of others is contrasted with the use of symbolic and anonymous names—"John Nobody," "John Blade," or simply "John"—to indicate the great mass of ordinary people with whom his sympathies lie. After the success of the Cuban Revolution, the interest in current affairs and Yankee political figures was complemented by the appearance of figures out of Cuba's revolutionary past and present (Antonio Maceo, José Martí, Fidel Castro, Che Guevara), with whom those less palatable individuals were contrasted. In *La paloma de vuelo popular*, the playful humor of Guillén's earliest works turned to irony and a wry sarcasm. In the *Elegías*, on the other hand, a sense of loss was added to the sense of outrage. These were in the main laments on the death of friends and victims or—as in "My Last Name"—for an entire history. In addition to the poet's usual stylistic vehicles, a variety of forms and meters were juxtaposed.

With the triumph of the Cuban Revolution, Guillén saw the fulfillment of his hopes and prophecies. He embraced the Revolution wholeheartedly, and its unfolding, along with the personalities who led it, immediately became a major theme of his poetry. The emotional tone of much of his verse also underwent a change that reflects the psychological, as well as the political and social, importance of the Revolution. The poet was filled with a new serenity, while the expressiveness of his poems reached a peak of revolutionary fervor. All this is manifest in *Tengo* (1964), and is nowhere more evident than in the poem that gives that book its title. Its very simplicity—"I Have" —already reflects the new sense of pride in and comradeship with the Cuban people. The new spirit of exuberance is unmistakable as the poem unfolds and Guillén's collective protagonist, at first surprised and bewildered by the sudden turn of events, is moved to take stock of his new relationship to reality. He concludes that he has finally come into possession of his birthright as a man: "I have, let's see:/ I have what was coming to me."

The old themes are still present, but Guillén's former combativeness has become focused on defending and spreading the influence and lessons of the Revolution. The enemy has not yet been completely defeated, and though Cuba is at last free the world as a whole is not and so Guillén still strikes familiar passionate chords of denunciation and exhortation (as in "It is all very well").

Guillén's celebration of the Cuban Revolution is more implicit in his latest collection of poems, *El gran zoo* (1967). By then the Revolution was an irrevocable fact of history, and from the perspective of that particular reality Guillén's witty little book treats the reader to an ironic interpretation of the contemporary—and particularly the capitalist—world which is now considered part of Cuba's bleak pre-history. Guillén therefore takes his audience on a tour of a symbolic zoo and introduces a mosaic of characters, animal, mineral, and vegetable, which reveal to the reader-tourist a vision of the universe in microcosm. The author's invitation to follow him through this menagerie, is not, however, entirely disinterested: on the one hand, we are invited to tour a zoo and see the "animals" in it; on the other hand, and more significantly, we are given a peculiarly Cuban tour of that zoo. More important than seeing just exactly what is caged is the realization that it is Cuba, and Guillén the guide, who are free and *not* caged and who interpret and reflect upon what *is*.

26

This is a volume which, in structure and style, is unique in Guillén's work. At the same time that the symbolic device of a zoo serves to create an organic totality, the poet moves away from the modes and forms of his previous works in favor of a stylized and elemental language in which everything is reduced to personification and metaphor. The lines are generally very short, the style clipped; rhyme is infrequent and the meter is inconsistent and at times reminiscent of free verse. The intent is to mimic the impersonal tone of plaques and of official notices and announcements, although alternating notes of pride, concern, amusement, and distaste creep into the comments of our host. The total effect of each of the poems is largely dependent on their interrelationship with each other and, although the great majority could stand alone, there are some which have no particular *raison d'être* except in terms of the book.

Guillén's major preoccupations are still present, although they are more pointedly synthesized: his uncompromising allegiance to Cuba and his rejection of a world ruled by greed and imperialist aggression are present in "The Caribbean," "The Usurers," and "The Eagles"; his concern for the total liberation of the Black man is clear in "Lynch" and "KKK"; implicit in "Tonton-Macoute" is the poet's revolutionary vision of a more humane world.

Guillén's work has, over the years, earned him numerous honors and prizes, including the Stalin Prize in 1953. He is currently President of the Unión Nacional de Escritores y Artistas Cubanos (UNEAC). He is also the editor-in-chief of *La Gaceta de Cuba,* an official cultural publication of the Unión, and sits on the editorial board of its literary magazine *Unión.* Since the triumph of the Revolution, he has held diplomatic posts for the Cuban government and traveled throughout Eastern Europe, China, and the Soviet Union.

His most recent poems, some of which have been published in various Cuban journals (and some of which I have included in this anthology), have been collected in a soon-to-be-published volume entitled *La rueda dentada* (The Serrated Wheel). It is clear from such poems as "I Declare Myself an Impure Man," "Problems of Underdevelopment," and "Propositions on the Death of Ana," that Guillén intends to continue writing, from a particularly Cuban perspective, a poetry which is explicit, deceptively simple in style, militant in its assumptions, one which reaches out to the Third World and looks forward to liberation, then peace.

A FINAL WORD

Several of the translations in this book have already appeared in magazines: "Problems of Underdevelopment" in the February 1970 issue of *Monthly Review*; and "Hunger," "Madrigal," "I Have," "The New Woman," "It Is All Very Well," and "I Declare Myself an Impure Man" in the Fall 1970 issue of the *Massachusetts Review*. The reader will also note that, with the exception of "Sensemayá," I have omitted from this collection the poems full of onomatopoeia and *jitanjáforas* typical of Guillén's work immediately prior to *West Indies, Ltd*. It is an omission I consider justified in a volume concerned primarily with Guillén's poetry of social protest and one which in no way hinders the introductory nature of this anthology.

In translating these poems I have tried to maintain the highest possible degree of fidelity to the meaning of the originals without at the same time betraying their aesthetic values. I have generally avoided the temptations of rhyme—which may appear a sacrilege when translating a poetry so rich in rhyme and tonal effects—but I have been very careful to adhere to Guillén's sense of meter and style. My central concern has been to remain faithful to the spirit and internal rhythms of the original poems. In this I believe I have on the whole been successful.

The majority of these translations were made during a period of approximately two months in the summer of 1969. Since that time they have been read and heard by people too numerous to mention. I would therefore like to take this opportunity to thank them all collectively. I would like particularly to thank Denah L. Lida, a teacher and friend since my undergraduate days at Brandeis, for her patience and her consistent encouragement; Bobbye Ortiz, Associate Editor of the *Monthly Review*, for her help in locating many of Guillén's latest poems and for the graciousness which has made her a valued friend; Liz Clauhsen, who served in lieu of a secretary; and David A. McMurray and Robert Crespi, *compañeros* who just by listening had some hand in this.

A final note of appreciation must of course go to Nicolás Guillén himself for authorizing the translations and permitting the reproduction of the Spanish originals, as well as for his humor, warmth, and friendship; and to Osmán Morote Best, in whose home, high in the Andes, I first heard the poet's verse: to both, *un hondo abrazo!*

—Robert Márquez

Cambridge, Massachusetts, August 1970
New York, April 1972

29

The Great Zoo / 1967

For Lea Lublin
who witnessed the birth
of these poems in Buenos Aires.

—N.G.

Aviso

Por un acuerdo del Ayuntamiento
fue creado este gran zoo
para nativos y extranjeros
y orgullo de nuestra nación.
Entre los ejemplares de más mérito
están los animales de agua y viento
(*como en el caso del ciclón*),
también un aconcagua verdadero,
una guitarra adolescente,
nubes vivas,
un mono catedrático y otro cotiledón.

¡Patria o muerte!

—El director

Announcement

By resolution of the municipality
this Great Zoo was created
for natives and foreigners
and the pride of the nation.
Among the specimens of greatest merit
are the animals of wind and water
(*as in the case of the Cyclone*),
also a genuine Aconcagua,
an adolescent guitar,
live clouds,
a professorial monkey and a monocotyledon.

Patria o muerte!

—*The Director*

Line 11 is a word play: the word *mono* in Spanish means both "one" and "monkey," depending on whether it is used as a prefix or a noun. The poet uses it as both.

El Caribe

En el acuario del Gran Zoo,
nada el Caribe.

       Este animal
marítimo y enigmático
tiene una cresta de cristal,
el lomo azul, la cola verde,
vientre de compacto coral,
grises aletas de ciclón.
En el acuario, esta inscripción:
              "Cuidado: muerde."

The Caribbean

In the aquarium of the Great Zoo,
swims the Caribbean.

  This seagoing
and enigmatic animal
has a crystal crescent,
a blue back, a green tail,
a belly of dense coral,
gray fins of cyclone speed.
In the aquarium, this inscription:
        "Beware: it bites."

 This poem, like several others included in this book, was first published in the poet's *Antología mayor*—Major Anthology (Havana: Bolsilibros Unión, 1964). These poems were intended as a kind of preview to *The Great Zoo*. The English version of this poem, unlike some of those that follow, corresponds exactly to the original and to the version which appears in the first edition of *El gran zoo*. In the second edition (February 1971) the fifth line reads: "has a white crystal crescent."

Guitarra

Fueron a cazar guitarras,
bajo la luna llena.
Y trajeron ésta,
pálida, fina, esbelta,
ojos de inagotable mulata,
cintura de abierta madera.
Es joven, apenas vuela.
Pero ya canta
cuando oye en otras jaulas
aletear sones y coplas.
Los sonesombre y las coplasolas.
Hay en su jaula esta inscripción:

"Cuidado: sueña."

Guitar

They went out hunting guitars
under the full moon
and brought back this one:
pale, elegant, shapely,
eyes of inexhaustible mulatta,
a waist of open wood.
She's young, she barely flies.
But already she sings
when she hears the flutter
of *sones* and couplets
in other cages.
The somber *sones* and the lonely couplets.
There is this inscription on her cage:
"Beware: she dreams."

In the original version of this poem, published in *Antología mayor*,
the sixth line described the guitar as having "a waist of glowing wood."
Sones, in line 10, is the plural of *son*.

Escarabajos

Vean los escarabajos.
El de la India,
vientre de terracota y alas de fieltro azul.
Los Gemelos, de cobre y gutapercha.
El Imperial de Holanda
originario de Sumatra (*cobre solo*).
El de lava volcánica
hallado en una tumba azteca.
El Gran Párpado de pórfido.

El de oro
(*donación especial de Edgar Poe*)
se nos murió.

Scarabs

These are the scarabs.
The one from India,
a terracotta belly and blue felt wings.
The Gemini, all copper and gutta-percha.
The Dutch Imperial one
originating in Sumatra (*copper only*).
The one of volcanic lava
was found in an Aztec tomb.
The Great Eyelid of jasper.

The gold one
(*a special donation of Edgar Poe*)
died on us.

La pajarita de papel

Sola, en su jaula mínima,
dormitando,
la pajarita de papel.

La Osa Mayor

Esta es la Osa Mayor.
Cazada en junio 4, 64,
por un sputnik cazador.
(*No tocar las estrellas
de la piel.*)

       Se solicita

un domador.

The Little Paper Bird

Alone, in its tiny cage,
napping,
the little paper bird.

Ursa Major

This is the Great Bear.
Captured June 4, 1964,
by a hunting sputnik.
(*Please do not touch
the stars on its skin.*)
                    Wanted: a trainer

First published in *Antología mayor*.

El Aconcagua

El Aconcagua. Bestia
solemne y frígida. Cabeza
blanca y ojos de piedra fija.
Anda en lentos rebaños
con otros animales semejantes
por entre rocallosos desamparos.

En la noche,
roza con belfo blando
las manos frías de la luna.

The Aconcagua

The Aconcagua. A solemn
and impassive beast. White
head and eyes of sturdy rock.
Travels in lazy herds
with animals like itself
through rocky desolation.

At night,
its soft lip nibbles
at the cold hands of the moon.

Originally published in *Antología mayor*. The title refers to the highest peak in South America, located in western Argentina. Height: 23,080 feet.

Los usureros

Monstruos ornitomorfos,
en anchas jaulas negras,
los usureros.

Hay el Copete Blanco (*Gran Usurero Real*)
y el Usurero-Buitre, de las grandes llanuras,
y el Torpedo Vulgar, que devora a sus hijos,
y el Rabidaga de cola cenicienta,
que devora a sus padres,
y el Vampiro Mergánsar,
que chupa sangre y vuela sobre el mar.

En el ocio forzado
de sus enormes jaulas negras,
los usureros cuentan y recuentan sus plumas
y se las prestan a interés.

The Usurers

Ornithomorphous monsters
in wide black cages,
the usurers.

There is the White Crested (*Great Royal Usurer*)
and the Buzzard Usurer, of the open plains,
and the Common Torpedo, that devours its offspring,
and the ash-colored Daggertail,
that devours its parents,
and the Vampire Merganser,
that sucks blood and flies over the ocean.

In the forced leisure
of their enormous black cages,
the usurers count and recount their feathers
and lend them to one another for a fee.

Los ríos

He aquí la jaula de las culebras.
Enroscados en sí mismos,
duermen los ríos, los sagrados ríos.
El Mississippi con sus negros,
el Amazonas con sus indios.
Son como los zunchos poderosos
de unos camiones gigantescos.

Riendo, los niños les arrojan
verdes islotes vivos,
selvas pintadas de papagayos,
canoas tripuladas
y otros ríos.

Los grandes ríos despiertan,
se desenroscan lentamente,
engullen todo, se hinchan, a poco más revientan,
y vuelven a quedar dormidos.

The Rivers

This is the cage of the serpents.
Coiled up on themselves,
the rivers, the sacred rivers, sleep.
The Mississippi with its Blacks.
The Amazon with its Indians.
They are like the mighty springs
on some gigantic trucks.

The children, laughing, toss them
live little green islands,
parrot-colored jungles,
manned canoes
and other rivers.

The bigger rivers awaken,
slowly unwind,
devour it all, swell up, almost to bursting,
and go to sleep again.

Originally published in *Antología mayor*.

Pesca

Esta señora inmensa
fue arponeada en la calle
y herida gravemente.

Sus pescadores arrojados
se prometían el aceite,
los bigotes delgados y flexibles,
la grasa . . . (*Descuartizarla sabiamente*).

Aquí está.

Convalece.

The Catch

This enormous lady
was harpooned in the street
and gravely wounded.

The daring fisherman who caught her
looked forward to her oil,
her slender and flexible down,
to her fat . . . (*to carving her skillfully*).

Here she is.

Convalescing.

This is the version published in the first edition of *Antología mayor.*
In the 1967 and 1971 versions, the title was changed to "Señora" and
the last line of the first stanza—"and gravely wounded"—was omitted.

Al Público:
AVIO-MAMUT

(*Nota al pie de una foto al aire libre, de 3½ metros de altura por 2 de ancho, que figura en el Gran Zoo*)

No era
la ruina de una avioneta,
como en un principio se creyó.
Era la osamenta
seca y abandonada de un mamut niño,
muerto en algún sitio de Siberia
y que un excursionista descubrió.

La avioneta es un desdentado,
y un gran sabio probó
que la osamenta tenía colmillos,
animal con más de un título
para estar en el Gran Zoo.

Pero como aquí
sólo se admiten seres vivos,
se ha dejado esta simple información,
con una foto de la pieza,
llamada *avio-mamut* de un modo ecléctico
para evitar cualquier otra discusión.

To the Public:
AERO-MAMMOTH

(A note at the foot of a photograph, 12 feet high and 6 feet wide, on display outside in the Great Zoo)

It was not
the wreck of a small airplane,
as originally was thought.
It was the dry,
abandoned skeleton
of a baby mammoth,
killed somewhere in Siberia
and discovered by an excursionist.

The small airplane is toothless,
and a great scholar has proved
that the skeleton had tusks,
an animal with more than one claim
to a place in the Great Zoo.

But since
we accept only living things,
this brief notice has been left here
with a photograph of the piece,
rather eclectically called *aero-mammoth*
to avoid any further discussion.

In the second (1971) edition of *El gran zoo* the first line of the second stanza has been altered to read: "The small airplane is a mechanical being . . ."

La sed

Esponja de agua dulce,
la Sed.
Espera un río, lo devora.
Absorbe un aguacero.
Estrangula
con una cinta colorada.
¡Atención! ¡Las gargantas!

Thirst

A sponge of sweet water,
Thirst.
It waits for a river, devours it.
It will absorb a downpour.
Strangles
with a scarlet ribbon.
Throats, take heed!

El hambre

Esta es el hambre. Un animal
todo colmillo y ojo.
Nadie le engaña ni distrae.
No se harta en una mesa.
No se contenta
con un almuerzo o una cena.
Anuncia siempre sangre.
Ruge como león, aprieta como boa,
piensa como persona.

El ejemplar que aquí se ofrece
fue cazado en la India (*suburbios de Bombay*),
pero existe en estado más o menos salvaje
en otras muchas partes.

No acercarse.

Hunger

This is hunger. An animal
all fangs and eyes.
It cannot be distracted or deceived.
It is not satisfied with one meal.
It is not content
with a lunch or a dinner.
Always threatens blood.
Roars like a lion, squeezes like a boa,
thinks like a person.

The specimen before you
was captured in India (*outskirts of Bombay*),
but it exists in a more or less savage state
in many other places.

Please stand back.

Institutriz

Catedrática
Enseña inglés y álgebra.

Oxford.

Ramonea
hojillas tiernas, altas.
Casta, mas relativamente.

(*Ama en silencio a un alumno elefante.*)

Nombre común: *jirafa.*

Governess

An instructor.
She teaches English and Algebra.

Oxford.

Browses among
high, tender little leaves.
Innocent, but only relatively so.

(She's secretly in love with a student elephant.)

Common name: *giraffe.*

Las nubes

El Nubario.
Capacidad: 84 nubes.
Una experiencia nueva, porque hay
nubes de todo el día,
y de muchos países diferentes.
(*La Dirección anuncia más.*)

Larguilenguas de pájaro,
rojizas,
las matutinas
hechas al poco sueño labrador
y a las albas vacías.
Detenidas,
de algodón seco y firme,
las matronales fijas del mediodía.
Como serpientes encendidas
las que anuncian a Véspero.
Curiosidad: Las hay de Uganda,
movidas por los vientos del gran lago Victoria.
Las del Turquino, bajas.
Las de los Alpes Marítimos.
Las del Pico Bolívar.
Negras, de gordas tetas,
las de tormenta.
También nubes románticas,
como por ejemplo las que empañan
el cielo del amor. Las coloreadas
de hace sesenta años
en los augurios de Noel.
Nubes con ángeles.

The Clouds

The nebulary.
Capacity: 84 clouds.
A new experience, for there are
clouds that last all day,
and come from many different lands.
(*The Director expects still more.*)

Reddish,
long-tongued like a bird,
the early morning clouds
made to the short sleep of the ploughman
and the empty dawns.
Quiescent,
of dry, firm cotton,
the matronly, immobile ones of noon.
Like flaming serpents
those announcing dusk.
A curiosity: there are some from Uganda,
driven by the winds off the great Lake Victoria.
Low clouds, those of *el Turquino*.
Those from the Maritime Alps.
Those from the Pico Bolívar.
Black, and full breasted,
the storm clouds.
Romantic clouds, as well,
for example those that drench
the skies with love. The rosy-colored clouds
on Christmas cards of
sixty years ago.
Clouds with angels on them.

Nubes con formas de titán,
de mapas conocidos (*Inglaterra*),
de kanguro, león.
En fin, un cargamento respetable.

Sin embargo,
las de raza *Polar*, rarísimas,
no hubo manera de traerlas vivas.
Llegaron en salmuera, expresamente
de Groenlandia, Noruega, Terranova.
(*La Dirección ha prometido
exhibirlas al público en vitrinas.*)

Clouds in the shape of titans,
known maps (*England*),
kangaroos, lions.
In short, a shipment worthy of note.

Still,
there was no way of bringing back alive
those very rare ones, of the *Polar* species.
They arrived in brine, directly
from Greenland, Norway, Newfoundland.
(*The Director has promised*
to put them in glass cages for public display.)

Line 19: *el Turquino* is the highest peak in the Sierra Maestra.

Los vientos

Usted no puede imaginar
cómo andaban estos vientos anoche.
Se les vio,
los ojos centelleantes,
largo y rígido el rabo.

Nada pudo desviarlos
(*ni oraciones ni votos*)
de una choza, de un barco solitario,
de una granja,
de todas esas cosas necesarias
que ellos destruyen sin saberlo.

Hasta que esta mañana los trajeron atados,
cogidos por sorpresa,
lentos enamorados,
cuando vagaban pensativos
junto a un campo de dalias.

(*Esos de allí, a la izquierda,
dormidos en sus cajas.*)

The Winds

You cannot imagine
how these winds behaved last night.
They were seen,
eyes flashing,
their tails long and rigid.

Nothing (*not prayers nor oaths*)
could turn them
from a hovel, from a lonely ship,
from a farmhouse,
from all those necessary things
that they unwittingly destroy.

They were finally brought back this morning, bound,
lingering lovers,
caught by surprise
while wandering pensively
near a field of dahlias.

(*Those over there, to the left,
asleep in their boxes.*)

In the second edition the last line reads: "asleep in their cages."

El tigre

Anda preso en su propia jaula
de duras rayas negras.
El metal con que ruge
quema, está al rojo blanco.

(*Un gangster.*
El instinto sexual.
Un boxeador.
Un furioso de celos.
Un general.
El puñal del amor.)

Tranquilizarse.
Un tigre
real.

The Tiger

He paces imprisoned in his own cage
of hard black stripes.
The metal with which he roars
burns, is white hot.

(*A gangster.*
The sexual instinct.
A boxer.
A jealousy-enraged lover.
A general.
The dagger of love.)

Please be calm.
It's a real
tiger.

Ciclón

Ciclón de raza,
recién llegado a Cuba de las islas Bahamas.
Se crió en Bermudas,
pero tiene parientes en Barbados.
Estuvo en Puerto Rico.
Arrancó de raíz el palo mayor de Jamaica.
Iba a violar a Guadalupe.
Logró violar a Martinica.

Edad: dos días.

Ave-Fénix

Esta es la jaula destinada
a la resurrección del Ave-Fénix.
(*En diciembre llegarán sus cenizas.*)

Cyclone

A thoroughbred cyclone,
recently arrived in Cuba from the Bahama Islands.
It was raised in Bermuda,
but has relatives in Barbados.
It has been to Puerto Rico.
It tore the great Jamaican palm up by the roots.
It was going to ravage Guadeloupe.
It succeeded in ravaging Martinique.

Age: two days.

The Phoenix

This is the cage reserved
for the resurrection of the Phoenix.
(*Its ashes will arrive in December.*)

Lynch

Lynch de Alabama.
Rabo en forma de látigo
y pezuñas terciarias.
Suele manifestarse
con una gran cruz en llamas.
Se alimenta de negros, sogas,
fuego, sangre, clavos,
alquitrán.

      Capturado
junto a una horca. Macho.
Castrado.

Lynch

Lynch of Alabama.
Tail in the form of a lash
and tertiary hooves.
Usually appears
with a great flaming cross.
Feeds on Negroes, ropes,
fire, blood, nails,
tar.

       Captured
at a hanging. Male.
Castrated.

El cangrejo

El terrible cangrejo que devora
senos, páncreas, próstatas,
hunde sus patas de insistencia fija
en un gran útero de plástico.
Destino limitado, pues no tiene
carne de estreno que morder,
linfa potable o sangre.

Tal vez no se ha querido
ofrecer todo el cuadro.
El Zoo, sin embargo,
brinda lo principal, ni más ni menos
que en otras importantes capitales.

A la derecha, junto al gangster.

Cancer

The terrible crab that devours
breasts, pancreae, prostate glands,
sinks fixedly insistent claws
into a great plastic uterus.
Its future is limited, for it lacks
choice meat to eat,
drinkable water or blood.

Part of the picture is
perhaps still missing.
The Zoo, however,
has what is important, neither more nor less
than other major capitals.

On the right, next to the gangster.

Gangster

Este pequeño gangster neoyorquino
es el hijo menor de un gangster de Chicago
y una madre *bull-dog*.

       Fue herido en el asalto
al Royal Bank de Seattle.
Chester.
Lucky.
Camel.
White Label o Four Roses.
Browning.
Heroína.
(*Sólo habla inglés*.)

Gangster

This little New York gangster
is the younger son of a gangster from Chicago
and a bulldog mother.

      He was wounded during the robbery
of the Royal Bank of Seattle.
Chesterfields.
Luckies.
Camels.
White Label or Four Roses.
A Browning.
Heroin.
(*Speaks only English.*)

KKK

Este cuadrúpedo procede
de Joplin, Misurí.
Carnicero.
Aúlla largamente en la noche
sin su dieta habitual de negro asado.

Acabará por sucumbir.
Un problema (*insoluble*) alimentarlo.

KKK

This quadruped originates
in Joplin, Missouri.
Carnivorous.
It howls long in the night
without its usual diet of roast Negro.

It will eventually succumb.
Feeding it is a(*n insoluble*) problem.

Las águilas

En esta parte están las águilas.
La caudal.
La imperial.
El águila en su nopal.
La bicéfala (*fenómeno*)
en una jaula personal.
Las condecoratrices
arrancadas del pecho de los condenados
en los fusilamientos.
La pecuniaria, doble, de oro $20 (*veinte dólares*).
Las heráldicas.
La prusiana, de negro siempre como una viuda fiel.
La que voló sesenta años sobre el Maine, en La Habana.
La yanqui, traída de Viet Nam.
Las napoleónicas y las romanas.
La celestial,
en cuyo pecho resplandece Altaír.
En fin,
el águila
de la leche condensada marca "El Aguila."
(*Un ejemplar
realmente original*.)

The Eagles

In this section, the eagles.
The red-tailed eagle.
The imperial eagle.
The eagle perched on a cactus.
The two-headed eagle (*a phenomenon*)
in a cage all by itself.
The decoration eagles
torn from the chests of those condemned
to execution.
The monetary eagle, doubled, $20 gold (*twenty dollars*).
The heraldic eagles.
The Prussian eagle, always dressed in black like a faithful
    widow.
The one that flew seventy years over the "Maine," in
    Havana.
The Yankee eagle, brought in from Vietnam.
The Napoleonic and Roman eagles.
The celestial eagle,
with Altair glittering on its breast.
Finally,
the eagle on Eagle Brand condensed milk.
(*A truly original
specimen.*)

Line 4: a reference to Mexico's heraldic symbol.

Line 5: a reference to the insignia of the Hapsburg emperors who, after Charles V, attempted to seal Spain off from the rest of Europe, thereby "protecting" it from exposure to "subversive" and "heretical" ideas.

Line 10: a reference to an early American coin called an Eagle and worth $10 in gold.

Line 13: a reference to the monument erected in Havana harbor in

Monos

El territorio de los monos.
De acuerdo con los métodos modernos
están en libertad provisional.

El de sombrero profesor.
Con su botella el del anís.
Los generales con sus sables de cola.
En su caballo estatua el héroe mono.
El mono oficinista en bicicleta.
Mono banquero en automóvil.
Decorado mono mariscal.
El monocorde cordio
fásico cotiledón.
Monosacárido.
Monoclinal.
Y todos esos otros que usted ve.

Para agosto
nos llegarán seiscientos monosmonos.
(*La monería fundamental.*)

---

memory of the U.S.S. "Maine," whose mysterious sinking in 1898 became the excuse for the beginning of the Spanish-American War. A hated symbol of American involvement in Cuban affairs, it was destroyed by the people of Cuba immediately after the triumph of their Revolution.

Line 17: Altair is a star of the first magnitude in the constellation Aquila.

Monkeys

This is the monkeys' territory.
In accordance with modern techniques
they are provisionally free.

The monkey wearing a professor's hat.
The anisette one with his bottle.
The generals with their saber tails.
The hero monkey on his statue horse.
The monkey public clerk on a bicycle.
The banker monkey in a car.
The decorated field marshal monkey.
The monochord heart
a monkey cotyledon in development.
The monosaccharide.
The monocline.
And all the others that you see.

In August
six hundred monkey-monkeys will arrive.
(*The essential mimics.*)

Line 5: a reference to "Anís del Mono," a brand of anisette very pop-
ular in Spain during the latter part of the nineteenth century.

Line 11 and the next three lines: a fairly literal interpretation of what,
in the original Spanish, is an untranslatable play on words that depends
for its effect on the ambiguity of *mono*—meaning both "one" and
"monkey." The poet begins with real monkeys, passes on to monkeys of
the human species, then to the "monkeys" of biology, chemistry, and
physics (all monkeys of the lexicon), and back to real monkeys—all with
slicing irony. This is typical of an inventive technique used throughout
the book and prefigured in the first poem, "Announcement."

Papaya

La papaya.
Animal
vegetal.
No es cierto
que conozca el pecado original.
Cuanto se diga,
mírenla,
es pura coincidencia. Sucia
literatura
que han padecido por igual
la calabaza y la sandía.
Cosas, en fin, de la abstinencia
(*senil o juvenil*)
sexual.

Papaya

The papaya.
A vegetable
animal.
It is untrue
that it has any knowledge of original sin.
Whatever may be said—
look at it—
is pure coincidence. Dirty
fantasies
to which the pumpkin and the watermelon
have also fallen victim.
The result, in short, of
(*senile or youthful*)
sexual abstinence.

This poem appears only in the second edition of *El gran zoo*. In Cuba, as in other Latin American countries, the word "papaya," not only denotes the fruit, but is also the euphemistic slang equivalent of vagina.

Luna

Mamífero metálico. Nocturno.

Se le ve
el rostro comido por un acné.

Sputniks y sonetos.

Moon

A metallic mammal. Nocturnal.

Its face
appears eaten by acne.

Sputniks and sonnets.

Tenor

Está el tenor en éxtasis
contemplando al tenor
del espejo, que es el mismo tenor
en éxtasis
que contempla al tenor.

Sale a veces a pasear por el mundo
llevado de un bramante de seda,
aplaudido en dólares,
tinta de imprenta
y otras sustancias gananciales.
(*Aquí en el zoo le molesta*
cantar por la comida
y no es muy generoso con sus arias.)

Milán Scala.
New York Metropolitan.
Opera de París.

Tenor

The tenor is in ecstasy
looking at the tenor
in the mirror, who is the same tenor
in ecstasy
looking at the tenor.

He occasionally goes for a walk around the world
led by a silken thread,
applauded with dollars,
printer's ink
and other lucrative substances.
(*Here in the zoo he is annoyed*
by having to sing for his food
and is not very generous with his arias.)

La Scala in Milan.
The New York Metropolitan.
The Paris Opera.

Policía

Este animal se llama policía.
Plantígrado soplador.
Variedades: la inglesa, *sherlock*. (*Pipa*.)
Carter, la norteamericana. (*Pipa*.)
Alimento normal:
pasto confidencial,
electrointerrogograbadoras,
comunismo (*internacional*),
noches agotadoras
de luz artificial.
Son mucho más pequeños los de raza *policeman*.
Metalbotones, chapa. La cabeza
formando gorra. Pelaje azul en general.
Alimento normal: delincuencia infantil,
disturbios, huelgas, raterías.
Comunismo (*local*).

Police

This animal is called police.
A whistling plantigrade.
Varieties: the English, *Sherlock*. (*Pipe*.)
The North American, *Carter*. (*Pipe*.)
Normal diet:
confidential fodder,
electrointerrogatingrecorders,
(*international*) Communism,
exhausting nights
of artificial light.
Those of the species *policeman* are much smaller.
Brass buttons, a badge. Head shaped like a cap.
Generally a blue coat.
Normal diet: juvenile delinquency,
disturbances, strikes, petty larceny,
(*local*) Communism.

El chulo

Orobotones en la camiseta
legítima H.R.
Rabocolt 38 con dril blanco espejo.
Cresta de jipijapa.
Mimí Pinsón en el pañuelo.

Echado en el fondo de la jaula
pasa su poca vida y gran hastío
de sueño en sueño con las secas putas
(*todas en estado cadavérico*)
del viejo santo San Isidro.

Nota: ejemplar único, cazado
hace sesenta años
una noche de riña con franceses
en Luz y Curazao.

Título: Tratante de blancas.
Verso 2: Marca de malla francesa.
Verso 4: Sombrero típico del Caribe.
Verso 10: Barrio de prostitución en La Habana.

The Pimp

Goldbuttons on his
genuine H&R vest.
Tailcolt .38, polished, and pressed drill.
Crest of *jipijapa*.
Handkerchief scented with Mimi Pinson.

Slouching in a corner of the cage,
his meagre life and too much boredom pass,
between sleeps, among the withered whores
(*everyone in a cadaverous state*)
of the old saint San Isidro.

Note: a unique specimen,
captured sixty years ago
during an evening brawl with Frenchmen
in Luz and Curaçao.

Line 2: H&R is a French trademark. (Author's note.)

Line 4: a *jipijapa* is a straw hat typical of the Caribbean, usually worn by dandies. (Author's note.)

Line 5: *Mimi Pinson* is apparently a reference to a cheap perfume, as well as to the name of the central character in a story by Alfred de Musset—the story of a young barmaid-washerwoman-doubling-as-prostitute who is as charitable and obliging as she is carefree.

Line 10: San Isidro was Havana's redlight district. (Author's note.)

Reloj

Quiróptero
de una paciencia extraordinaria
no exenta de crueldad,
sobre todo
con los ajedrecistas y los novios.

Sin embargo,
es cordial a las 3 menos 1/4
tanto como a las 9 y 15, los únicos momentos
en que estaría dispuesto a darnos un abrazo.

Clock

A bat
of extraordinary patience
not lacking in cruelty,
especially
with chess players and lovers.

Yet
it is cordial at a quarter-to-three
as well as at nine-fifteen, the only times
it would be willing to embrace us.

Aviso:
GRAN ZOO DE LA HABANA

*Museo de prehistoria abierto al público.—Todos los días
menos los domingos.—Idiomas: español, inglés, y ruso.*

Se avisa la llegada
de nuevos ejemplares, a saber:
La gran paloma fósil del jurásico
en la que son visibles todavía
sus dos dispositivos lanzabombas.
Hay una colección de hachas atómicas,
máscaras rituales de forma antiaerolítica
y macanas de sílex radioactivo.
Finalmente, un avión
(*el tan buscado caza del plioceno*)
que es una pieza de excepción.

¡Patria o muerte!

—*El director*

Announcement:
GREAT ZOO OF HAVANA

Prehistoric museum open to the public.—Daily except Sunday.—Languages: Spanish, English, and Russian.

We would like to announce the arrival
of new specimens, to wit:
The great bird fossil of the Jurassic period
whose two rocket-launching pads
are still visible.
There is a collection of atomic axes,
ritual masks of the anti-atmospheric type,
and clubs of radioactive silex.
Finally, an airplane
(*the much sought after predator
of the Pliocene epoch*)
which is an exceptional piece.

Patria o muerte!

—The Director

In the second edition the phrase "Patria o muerte!" has been changed to read: "Havana, June 5."

Oradores

Aquí los oradores.
Algunos son campeones
provinciales. Otros
lo son olímpicos. Otros
no son nada, ni siquiera oradores.

Plumaje muy diverso.
Con todo, predomina
cierta *nuance* vulgar del amarillo.
Como usted nota,
la confusión es colosal.

> *Señoras y señores*
> *¡Camaradas!*
> *Amados hijos míos*
> *Señor Presidente, señores diputados*
> *Respetable público*
> *¡Compañeros!*
> *Me siento emocionado*
> *Es ésta la primera vez*
> *Esta noche no debéis esperar de mi un discurso*
> *Permitidme que*
> *No sé cómo yo oso*
> *¡Qué distinta es, esclarecido Cristóbal Colón,*
> *Los familiares del difunto*

Cuando al fin enronquecen hacen gárgaras
con las palabras que les sobran
(*muy pocas*)
y recomienzan la función,

Orators

Here the orators.
Some are champions
from the provinces. Others
are Olympic champions. Others
are nothing, not even orators.

Their plumage is very different.
Still, a certain vulgar nuance
of yellow predominates.
As you can see,
the confusion is colossal.

> *Ladies and gentlemen*
> *Comrades!*
> *My beloved children*
> > *Mr. President, esteemed delegates*
>
> *Honored guests*
> *Compañeros!*
> *I am moved*
> *This is the first time*
> *You must not expect me to give a speech tonight*
> *Allow me to*
> *I don't know how I dare to*
> *How very different! Noble Christopher Colum-*
> > *bus,*
>
> *The family of the deceased*

When they finally become hoarse, they gargle
with the surplus words
(*a very few*)
and resume the ceremony,

y señores maradas
esperar de mí un discurso
jos míos respetable
cionado
funto cómo yo oso
Colón.

and gentlemen rades
to give a speech tonight
ved children honored
oved
ceased how I dare to
Columbus.

Line 18: this line was eliminated in the second edition of *El gran zoo*.

El sueño

Esta mariposa nocturna
planea sobre nuestra cabeza
como el buitre sobre la carroña.
(*El ejemplar*
que aquí exhibimos es el sueño vulgar.)

Sin embargo,
la dirección promete para fines de año,
o más pronto, tal vez,
remesas escogidas de sueños
así en hombre como en mujer.

Cinco cajas de moscas tsé-tsé
fueron pedidas anteayer.

Dream

This nocturnal butterfly
glides around our heads
like a buzzard above carrion.
(*The specimen
on exhibit here is the common dream.*)

But,
we expect by the year's end
or sooner, perhaps,
a select shipment of dreams,
male and female.

Five boxes of tsetse flies
were ordered the day before yesterday.

Gorila

El gorila es un animal
a poco más enteramente humano.
No tiene patas sino casi pies,
no tiene garras sino casi manos.
Le estoy hablando a usted
del gorila del bosque africano.

El animal que está a la vista,
a poco más
es un gorila enteramente.
Patas en lugar de pies
y casi garras en lugar de manos.
Le estoy mostrando a usted
el gorila americano.

Lo adquirió
nuestro agente viajero en un cuartel
para el Gran Zoo.

Gorilla

The gorilla is an animal
nearly completely human.
It has no paws but feet almost.
It has no claws but hands almost.
I am speaking of
the gorilla of the African forest.

The animal before you
is nearly
completely gorilla.
It has paws instead of feet
and claws almost instead of hands.
I show you
the American gorilla.

It was acquired in a barracks
by our traveling representative
for the Great Zoo.

Tonton-Macoute

a René Depestre

Cánido
numeroso en Haití bajo la Era
Cuadrúpeda.
        Ejemplar
hallado en el corral presidencial
junto a las ruinas
silvestres de palacio.
(*Port-au-Prince.*)

Perdió la pata izquierda de un balazo
frente al Champ de Mars
en un tumulto popular.

Morirá en breves días
a causa de la herida de machete
que le hunde el frontal.

Se le está preparando una vitrina
en el museo de historia natural.

Tonton-Macoute

for René Depestre

A Canidae
flourishing in Haiti during the
Quadruped Era.
    Specimen
found in the presidential corral
next to the wild
ruins of the palace.
(*Port-au-Prince.*)

It lost its left leg to a bullet
in front of the Champ de Mars
during a popular uprising.
It will die shortly
as a result of the machete wound
rending its forehead.

A showcase is being prepared for it
in the Museum of Natural History.

Bomba atómica

Esta es la bomba. Mírenla.
Reposa dormitando. Por favor
no provocarla
con bastones, varillas, palos, pinchos,
piedras. Prohibido
arrojarle alimentos.
¡Cuidado con las manos,
los ojos!

(La Dirección
lo ha dicho y advertido,
pero nadie hace caso,
ni siquiera el Ministro.)

Es un peligro bárbaro
este animal aquí.

104

Atomic Bomb

This is the bomb. Look at it.
It's napping. Please
do not provoke it
with canes, rods, sticks, thorns,
rocks. Feeding
is prohibited.
Careful with your hands,
your eyes!

(The Director
has said it and given notice,
but no one pays any attention,
not even the Minister.)

A very great danger
this animal here.

La Estrella Pólar

Se descongela sin remedio
la Estrella Polar.
Diez millones, y aún más
diarios de toneladas
(*hielo, luz fría, gas*)
pierde de su estructura
este inmenso animal.

En los sitios vacíos
verán,
miren ustedes hacia allá,
cómo nuestro equipo restaurador
va colocando masas de algodón.
Pero eso no puede bastar
y dentro de cuatro años a lo sumo
los navegantes tendrán
que andar a tientas por el mar.

¡Qué responsabilidad!
El animal que más nos cuesta
y el que menos se puede conservar.

The Pole Star

The Pole Star
melts irrevocably.
Ten million tons
(*ice, cold light, gas*)
and even more is daily
lost from the frame
of this immense animal.

If you look over there,
you will see
how our restoration team
is placing masses of cotton
in the empty spaces.
But that is not enough
and within four years at most
navigators will be forced
to grope their way over dark seas.

What a responsibility!
The animal that costs us most
and the one we are least able to preserve.

Line 14: in the second edition, this has been changed to read: "and within four centuries at most."

Salida

Aquí termina la visita de hoy.
Mañana será otro día
y volveremos al Gran Zoo.

Seguir la flecha
Al fondo (*izquierda*)
SALIDA
EXIT
SORTIE

Exit

Here ends the visit for today.
Tomorrow is another day
and we'll return to the Great Zoo.

Follow the arrow
at the back (*to the left*)
SALIDA
EXIT
SORTIE

Other Poems / 1925-1969

La nueva musa

Antes, el poeta era un músico
que frente a la orquesta daba saltos
e imantaba con su batuta
los suspiros de la flauta,
el violín pedigüeño,
los bajos, roncos como unos abuelos
y hasta el tambor inmodesto.
El poeta se embriagaba
en medio del estruendo.
Ahora, el poeta se mete dentro de sí mismo
y allá dentro, dirige su orquesta.

The New Muse

The poet, once, was a musician
who danced before the orchestra
and lured with his baton
the sighs of the flute,
the importunate violin,
the bass, hoarse as a grandfather,
and even the immodest drum.
He got drunk
amid the clamor.
The poet, now, withdraws into himself
and there, within, conducts his orchestra.

WAYNESBURG COLLEGE LIBRARY
WAYNESBURG, PA.

Lluvia

Bajo el cielo plomizo
de la tarde lluviosa,
llora el agua con lágrima
monótona.

Miro tras los cristales
las ramas temblorosas
enjoyarse con sartas
de gotas.

Se desbordó el arroyo,
inundó cuatro chozas.
(A mí me sobresalta la odisea de esta hormiga,
ahogada en una rosa.)

Rain

Under the leaden sky
of the rainy afternoon,
the water weeps with a
monotonous tear.

Through the windows I can see
the trembling branches
bejeweled with beads
of rain drops.

The stream has flooded
and overturned four shacks.
(I startle at the odyssey of an ant
drowned in a rose.)

Si a mí me hubieran dicho . . .

Si a mí me hubieran dicho
que iba a llegar el día
en que los dos no fuéramos
más que simples amigos,
no lo hubiera creído.

Que alguien nos viera, digo,
hablar indiferentes
del sol o de la lluvia
como simples amigos,
no lo hubiera creído.

¡Ay! qué puñal tan fino
éste de cuya herida
me muero y me desangro . . .
Si me lo hubieran dicho,
no lo hubiera creído.

If anyone had told me . . .

If anyone had told me
that there would come a day
when we two would not be
more than simply friends,
I wouldn't have believed it.

That someone would see us, say,
talking indifferently
about the sun, about the rain
like two friends simply,
I wouldn't have believed it.

Oh, what a fine dagger this
from whose wound I bleed and die . . .
If anyone had told me,
I would not have believed it.

Reloj

Me gustan ciertas horas, como las 3 menos cuarto,
porque el reloj parece que tiene
esa actitud fraterna, acogedora,
del que va a darnos un abrazo.

Aunque también el Tiempo, así, es un Cristo en agonía
que por la herida del costado
va desangrándose sutilmente
entre el Futuro y el Pasado.

The Clock

I like certain hours, like a quarter-to-three,
because the clock seems then to have
the warm, fraternal attitude
of someone about to hug us.

Though Time, like that, is also a Christ in agony
bleeding slowly
from his wounded side
between the Future and the Past.

Bares

Amo los bares y tabernas
junto al mar,
donde la gente charla y bebe
sólo por beber y charlar.
Donde Juan Nadie llega y pide
su trago elemental,
y están Juan Bronco y Juan Navaja
y Juan Narices y hasta Juan
Simple, el sólo, el simplemente
Juan.

Allí la blanca ola
bate de la amistad;
una amistad de pueblo, sin retórica,
una ola de ¡hola! y ¿cómo estás?
Allí huele a pescado,
a mangle, a ron, a sal
y a camisa sudada puesta a secar al sol.

Búscame, hermano, y me hallarás
(en La Habana, en Oporto,
en Jacmel, en Shanghai)
con la sencilla gente
que sólo por beber y charlar
puebla los bares y tabernas
junto al mar.

Bars

I love those bars and taverns
by the sea,
where people chat and drink
merely to drink and chat.
Where John Nobody goes and asks
for his favorite drink,
where you'll find John Rowdy and John Blade
and John Nosey and even John
Simple, that's all, simply
John.

There the white wave
foams in friendship,
the friendship of the people, without rhetoric,
a wave of "Hey there!" and "How ya doin'?"
There it smells of fish,
of mangroves, of rum, of salt,
and sweaty shirts hung in the sun to dry.

Look for me, brother, and you will find me
(in Havana, in Oporto,
in Jacmel, in Shanghai)
with the ordinary people
who merely to drink and chat,
fill the bars and taverns
by the sea.

Epitafio para Lucía

a Jesualdo

Murió callada y provincial. Tenía
llenos los ojos de paz fría,
de lluvia lenta y lenta melodía.
Su voz, como un cristal esmerilado,
anunciaba un resplandor encerrado.
Se llamó, la llamaban vagamente Lucía.
(En este breve mármol ha quedado
toda su biografía.)

An Epitaph for Lucía

for Jesualdo

She died in silence and provincially. Her eyes
were full of frigid peace,
of silent falling rain and a slow melody.
Her voice, like a ground-glass window,
hinted at a secluded splendor.
Her name was, she was vaguely called Lucía.
(All her biography has been preserved
on this small slab of marble.)

Futuro

Acaso vengan otros hombres
(blancos o negros, para el caso es igual),
más poderosos, más resueltos,
que por el aire o sobre el mar
nos desbaraten nuestros aeroplanos
y nos impongan su verdad.

¡Quisiera ver a los americanos!
Ellos, que nos humillan con su fuerza,
modernos incas, nuevos aztecas, ¿qué harán?
Como los viejos indios, trabajarían
en las minas para el nuevo español,
sin pershing y sin lindbergh
y hasta sin nueva york,
comiendo sanduiches con los conquistadores
y empujándolos en sus rolls-royces.

The Future

Perhaps other men will come
(white men or Black, it's all the same),
more powerful, more resolute,
who in the air and on the sea
will obliterate our airplanes
and impose on us their truth.

I'd like to see the Americans then!
They, who bend us with their might,
modern Incas, new Aztecs, what will they do?
Like the ancient Indians, they would work
the mines for the new Spaniard,
without Pershing and without Lindbergh
and even without New York,
eating sandwiches with the conqueror
and driving him around in their Rolls Royces.

El aeroplano

Cuando pase esta época
y se queme en la llama de los siglos
toda nuestra documentación humana;
cuando no exista ya la clave
de nuestro progreso actual
y con la paciencia del que no sabe
el hombre tenga que volver a empezar,
entonces aparecerán
rasgos de nuestra muerta civilización.
¿Qué dirán los naturalistas del futuro
ante una armazón de aeroplano
desenterrada en cualquier llanura,
o en la cumbre de una montaña,
mohosa, fosilizada,
monumental, incomprensible, extraña?
De seguro que harán
muchísimos aspavientos
y clasificarán el aeroplano
entre los ejemplares de una fauna extinguida.

The Airplane

When this age has passed
and all our human documents
have been consumed by the flame of centuries;
when the key to all our current progress
no longer exists
and with the patience of the ignorant
man has to begin again,
then vestiges
of our dead civilization will appear.
What will the naturalists of the future say
faced with the skeleton of an airplane
unearthed on a plain
or on a mountain top,
rusty, fossilized,
monumental, incomprehensible, strange?
They will no doubt be
very much amazed
and will classify the airplane
among the specimens of an extinct fauna.

Balada

Ay, venga, paloma, venga
y cuénteme usted su pena.

—Pasar he visto a dos hombres
armados y con banderas;
el uno en caballo moro,
el otro en potranca negra.
Dejaron casa y mujer,
partieron a lueñes tierras;
el odio los acompaña,
la muerte en las manos llevan.
¿A dónde váis, preguntéles,
y ambos a dos respondieran:
Vamos andando, paloma,
andando para la guerra.
Así dicen, y después
con ocho pezuñas vuelan,
vestidos de polvo y sol,
armados y con banderas,
el uno en caballo moro,
el otro en potranca negra.
Ay, venga, paloma, venga
y cuénteme usted su pena.

—Pasar he visto a dos viudas
como jamás antes viera,
pues que de una misma lágrima
estatuas parecen hechas.
¿A dónde váis, mis señoras?
pregunté a las dos al verlas.

Ballad

Come, dove, oh dove, come
tell me the tale of your woe.

I've seen two men passing
with guns and with flags;
the one rode a pinto,
the other a black mare.
For remote lands they left
their houses and wives,
with hate as their escort,
bearing death in their hands.
I asked "Where are you going?"
and both spoke at once:
"Dove, we go riding,
go riding to war,"
so they say, then
on eight hooves they fly,
dressed in dust and in sun,
with guns and with flags,
one rides a pinto
the other a black mare.
Come, dove, oh dove, come
tell me the tale of your woe.

I've seen widows passing
like no two I've seen;
they are like two statues
formed of one single tear.
"Where are you going,
my ladies?" I asked.

129

Vamos por nuestros maridos,
paloma, me respondieran.
De su partida y llegada
tenemos amargas nuevas;
tendidos están y muertos,
muertos los dos en la hierba,
gusanos ya sobre el vientre
y buitres en la cabeza,
sin fuego las armas mudas
y sin aire las banderas;
se espantó el caballo moro,
huyó la potranca negra.

Ay, venga, paloma, venga
y cuénteme usted su pena.

"We go for our husbands,
oh dove," they replied.
"Of their going and coming
bitter tidings we have;
they are laid out and dead now,
both dead on the grass,
maggots feast on their stomachs,
buzzards perch on their heads,
their silent guns fireless
and their flags without air;
the pinto horse panicked,
the black mare she fled.

Come, dove, oh dove, come
tell me the tale of your woe.

Sensemayá

Canto para matar una culebra

¡Mayombe—bombe—mayombé!
¡Mayombe—bombe—mayombé!
¡Mayombe—bombe—mayombé!

La culebra tiene los ojos de vidrio;
la culebra viene y se enreda en un palo;
con sus ojos de vidrio, en un palo,
con sus ojos de vidrio.
La culebra camina sin patas;
la culebra se esconde en la yerba;
caminando se esconde en la yerba,
caminando sin patas.

¡Mayombe—bombe—mayombé!
¡Mayombe—bombe—mayombé!
¡Mayombe—bombe—mayombé!

Tú le das con el hacha, y se muere:
¡dale ya!
¡No le des con el pie, que te muerde,
no le des con el pie, que se va!

Sensemayá, la culebra,
sensemayá.
Sensemayá, con sus ojos,
sensemayá.
Sensemayá, con su lengua,
sensemayá.

Sensemayá

Chant for killing a snake

Mayombe—bombe—mayombé!
Mayombe—bombe—mayombé!
Mayombe—bombe—mayombé!

The serpent has eyes made of glass;
the serpent comes, wraps itself round a stick;
with its eyes made of glass, round a stick,
with its eyes made of glass.
The serpent walks without any legs;
the serpent hides in the grass;
walking hides in the grass,
walking without any legs.

Mayombe—bombe—mayombé!
Mayombe—bombe—mayombé!
Mayombe—bombe—mayombé!

Hit it with the ax, and it dies:
hit it now!
Don't hit it with your foot, it will bite you,
Don't hit it with your foot, it will flee!

Sensemayá, the serpent,
sensemayá.
Sensemayá, with his eyes,
sensemayá.
Sensemayá, with his tongue,
sensemayá.

133

Sensemayá, con su boca,
sensemayá.

La culebra muerta no puede comer;
la culebra muerta no puede silbar;
no puede caminar,
no puede correr.
La culebra muerta no puede mirar;
la culebra muerta no puede beber;
no puede respirar,
no puede morder.

¡Mayombe—bombe—mayombé!
Sensemayá, la culebra . . .
¡Mayombe—bombe—mayombé!
Sensemayá, no se mueve . . .
¡Mayombe—bombe—mayombé!
Sensemayá, la culebra . . .
¡Mayombe—bombe—mayombé!
¡Sensemayá, se murió!

Sensemayá, with his mouth,
sensemayá.

The dead serpent cannot eat;
the dead serpent cannot hiss;
cannot walk,
cannot run.
The dead serpent cannot see;
the dead serpent cannot drink;
cannot breathe,
cannot bite!

Mayombe—bombe—mayombé!
Sensemayá, the serpent . . .
Mayombe—bombe—mayombé!
Sensemayá, is not moving . . .
Mayombe—bombe—mayombé!
Sensemayá, the serpent . . .
Mayombe—bombe—mayombé!
Sensemayá, he is dead!

Son número 6

Yoruba soy, lloro en yoruba
lucumí.
Como soy un yoruba de Cuba,
quiero que hasta Cuba suba mi llanto yoruba:
que suba el alegre llanto yoruba
que sale de mí.

Yoruba soy,
cantando voy,
llorando estoy,
y cuando no soy yoruba,
soy congo, mandinga, carabalí.
Atiendan, amigos, mi son que empieza así:
> Adivinanza
> de la esperanza:
> lo mío es tuyo,
> lo tuyo es mío;
> toda la sangre
> formando un río.

La ceiba ceiba con su penacho;
el padre padre con su muchacho;
la jicotea en su carapacho.
¡Que rompa el son caliente,
y que lo baile la gente,
pecho con pecho,
vaso con vaso
y agua con agua con aguardiente!

Yoruba soy, soy lucumí,
mandinga, congo, carabalí.

Son Number 6

I'm Yoruba, weep in Yoruba
Lucumi.
Since I'm a Yoruba from Cuba,
I want to raise up to Cuba my weep in Yoruba:
the happy weep in Yoruba
that comes out of me.

I'm Yoruba,
singing,
weeping,
and when I'm not a Yoruba,
I'm Congo, Mandingo, Carabali.
Listen, friends, to my *son*: its start will be:
> A riddle
> the scope
> of hope:
> what's mine is yours,
> what's yours is mine;
> all the blood
> forming one river.

The silk-cotton tree silk-cotton tree with pennant;
the father a father to his son;
the tortoise hidden in its shell.
Let the wild *son* burst,
and the people dance,
chest to chest,
glass to glass
and water on water with brandy!

I'm Yoruba, I'm Lucumi,
Mandingo, Congo, Carabali.

Atiendan, amigos, mi son, que sigue así:
    Estamos juntos desde muy lejos,
    jóvenes, viejos,
    negros y blancos, todo mezclado;
    uno mandando y otro mandado,
    todo mezclado;
    San Berenito y otro mandado,
    todo mezclado;
    negros y blancos desde muy lejos,
    todo mezclado;
    Santa María y uno mandado,
    todo mezclado;
    todo mezclado, Santa María,
    San Berenito, todo mezclado,
    todo mezclado, San Berenito,
    San Berenito, Santa María.
    Santa María, San Berenito,
    ¡todo mezclado!

Yoruba soy, soy lucumí,
mandinga, congo, carabalí.
Atiendan, amigos, mi son, que acaba así:
    Salga el mulato,
    suelte el zapato,
    díganle al blanco que no se va . . .
    De aquí no hay nadie que se separe;
    mire y no pare,
    oiga y no pare,
    beba y no pare,
    coma y no pare,
    viva y no pare,
    ¡que el son de todos no va a parar!

Listen, friends, to my *son*: what's next you'll see:
        We've been together since long ago,
        young, old,
        white and black, all mixed;
        one commanding, another sent,
        all mixed;
        San Berenito and another sent,
        all mixed;
        black and white since long ago,
        all mixed;
        Santa María and another sent,
        all mixed;
        all mixed, Santa María,
        San Berenito, all mixed,
        all mixed, San Berenito,
        San Berenito, Santa María.
        Santa María, San Berenito,
        all mixed!

I'm Yoruba, I'm Lucumi,
Mandingo, Congo, Carabali.
Listen, friends, to my *son*: its end will be:
        Come out mulatto,
        loosen your shoe,
        tell the white man he's not leaving . . .
        no one cuts himself off from here;
        look and don't stop,
        hear and don't stop,
        drink and don't stop,
        eat and don't stop,
        live and don't stop,
        for everyone's *son* is not going to stop.

Mujer nueva

Con el círculo ecuatorial
ceñido a la cintura como a un pequeño mundo,
la negra, mujer nueva,
avanza en su ligera bata de serpiente.

Coronada de palmas
como una diosa recién llegada,
ella trae la palabra inédita,
el anca fuerte,
la voz, el diente, la mañana y el salto.

Chorro de sangre joven
bajo un pedazo de piel fresca,
y el pie incansable
para la pista profunda del tambor.

The New Woman

With the equatorial circle
tied around her waist like a little world,
the Negress, the new woman,
comes forward in her airy serpent morning gown.

Crowned with palms
like a newly arrived goddess,
she brings unspoken words,
her solid loins,
her voice, her teeth, the morning and her leap.

A rush of youthful blood
beneath a piece of skin that's fresh,
and tireless feet
for the deep rhythm of the drum.

Madrigal

De tus manos gotean
las uñas, en un manojo de diez uvas moradas.

Piel,
carne de tronco quemado,
que cuando naufraga en el espejo, ahuma
las algas tímidas del fondo.

Madrigal

From your hands fall, drop by drop,
your fingernails, a cluster of ten purple grapes.

Skin,
scorched tree-trunk flesh,
that sinking in the mirror cures in smoke
the timid seaweed in its depths.

Madrigal

Tu vientre sabe más que tu cabeza
y tanto como tus muslos.

Esa
es la fuerte gracia negra
de tu cuerpo desnudo.

Signo de selva el tuyo,
con tus collares rojos,
tus brazaletes de oro curvo,
y ese caimán oscuro
nadando en el Zambeze de tus ojos.

Madrigal

Your womb is smarter than your head,
smart as your thighs.

That's
the fierce black grace
of your naked body.

Yours is the symbol of the forest,
with your red necklaces,
your bracelets of curved gold,
and that dark alligator
swimming in the Zambezi of your eyes.

Madrigal

Sencilla y vertical,
como una caña en el cañaveral.

Oh retadora del furor
genital:
tu andar fabrica para el espasmo gritador
espuma equina entre tus muslos de metal.

Madrigal

Unadorned and vertical
as a canestalk in the canefield.

Oh, taunter of genital
fury:
your walk yields for the screaming spasm
equine spume between your metal thighs.

Guadalupe, W.I.

Pointe-à-Pitre

Los negros, trabajando
junto al vapor. Los árabes, vendiendo,
los franceses, paseando y descansando,
y el sol, ardiendo.
En el puerto se acuesta
el mar. El aire tuesta
las palmeras . . . Yo grito: ¡Guadalupe!
pero nadie contesta.

Parte el vapor, arando
las aguas impasibles con espumoso estruendo.
Allá, quedan los negros trabajando,
los árabes vendiendo,
los franceses paseando y descansando,
y el sol ardiendo . . .

Guadeloupe, W.I.

Pointe-à-Pitre

The Blacks, by the ship,
working. The Arabs, selling,
the French, strolling and resting,
and the sun, scorching.
The sea rides in to lie
at port. The air toasts
the palm trees . . . I scream: "Guadeloupe!"
but no answer.

The ship weighs anchor, ploughing
the impassive waters with a foamy thunder.
Behind it, the Blacks keep working,
the Arabs selling,
the French strolling and resting,
and the sun scorching . . .

Caña

El negro
junto al cañaveral.

El yanqui
sobre el cañaveral.

La tierra
bajo el cañaveral.

¡Sangre
que se nos va!

Sugarcane

The Black
next to the cane.

The Yankee
over the canefield.

The earth
under the canefield.

The blood
we are losing!

Adivinanzas

En los dientes, la mañana,
y la noche en el pellejo.
¿Quién será, quién no será?
                            —El negro.

Con ser hembra y no ser bella,
harás lo que ella te mande.
¿Quién será, quién no será?
                            —El hambre.

Esclava de los esclavos,
y con los dueños, tirana.
¿Quién será, quién no será?
                            —La caña.

Escándalo de una mano
que nunca ignora la otra.
¿Quién será, quién no será?
                            —La limosna.

Un hombre que está llorando
con la risa que aprendió.
¿Quién será, quién no será?
                            —Yo.

Riddles

In his teeth, the morning,
and in his skin, the night.
Who is it? Who is it not?
                    —The Negro.

Though a woman and not pretty,
you'll do what she commands.
Who is it? Who is it not?
                    —Hunger.

Slave of the slaves
and of the masters, tyrant.
Who is it? Who is it not?
                    —Sugarcane.

Scandal of the one hand
which never forgets the other.
Who is it? Who is it not?
                    —Alms.

A man who is crying
with a smile that he once learned.
Who is it? Who is it not?
                    —Me.

Sabás

Yo vi a Sabás, el negro sin veneno,
pedir su pan de puerta en puerta.
¿Por qué, Sabás, la mano abierta?
(Este Sabás es un negro bueno.)

Aunque te den el pan, el pan es poco,
y menos ese pan de puerta en puerta.
¿Por qué, Sabás, la mano abierta?
(Este Sabás es un negro loco.)

Yo vi a Sabás, el negro hirsuto,
pedir por Dios para su muerta.
¿Por qué, Sabás, la mano abierta?
(Este Sabás es un negro bruto.)

Coge tu pan, pero no lo pidas;
coge tu luz, coge tu esperanza cierta
como a un caballo por las bridas.
Plántate en medio de la puerta,
pero no con la mano abierta,
ni con tu cordura de loco:
aunque te den el pan, el pan es poco,
y menos ese pan de puerta en puerta.

¡Caramba, Sabás, que no se diga!
¡Sujétate los pantalones,
y mira a ver si te las compones
para educarte la barriga!
La muerte, a veces, es buena amiga,
y el no comer, cuando es preciso

Sabás

I saw Sabás, the unembittered Black,
beg his bread from door to door.
Why, Sabás, with an open hand?
(This Sabás is a good Negro.)

Even if they give you bread, it is too little,
and less this bread from door to door.
Why, Sabás, with an open hand?
(This Sabás is a crazy Negro.)

I saw Sabás, the rugged Black,
beg in God's name for the departed.
Why, Sabás, with an open hand?
(This Sabás is a stupid Negro.)

Take your bread, but don't beg for it;
seize your dawn, seize your certain hope
as you would a stallion by the bridle.
Plant yourself in the middle of the doorway,
but not with the open hand extended,
nor with your madman's commonsense:
even if they give you bread, it is too little,
and less this bread from door to door.

Caramba, Sabás, don't let 'em say it!
Tighten up your belt
and see if you can manage
to educate your stomach!
Death is, at times, a welcome friend,
and not to eat submissive bread,

para comer, el pan sumiso,
tiene belleza. El cielo abriga.
El sol calienta. Es blando el piso
del portal. Espera un poco,
afirma el paso irresoluto
y afloja más el freno . . .
¡Caramba, Sabás, no seas tan loco!
¡Sabás, no seas tan bruto,
ni tan bueno!

when one just has to eat,
has beauty. The sky is nourishing.
The sun is warm. The doorway floor
is soft. Just wait a bit,
assert the irresolute step
and loosen up your reins . . .
Caramba, Sabás, don't be so crazy!
Sabás, don't be so stupid,
nor so good!

Sudor y látigo

Látigo,
sudor y látigo.

El sol despertó temprano
y encontró al negro descalzo,
desnudo el cuerpo llagado,
sobre el campo.

Látigo,
sudor y látigo.

El viento pasó gritando:
—¡Qué flor negra en cada mano!
La sangre le dijo: ¡vamos!
El dijo a la sangre: ¡vamos!
Partió en su sangre, descalzo.
El cañaveral, temblando,
le abrió paso.

Después, el cielo callado,
y bajo el cielo, el esclavo
tinto en la sangre del amo.

Látigo,
sudor y látigo,
tinto en la sangre del amo;
látigo,
sudor y látigo,
tinto en la sangre del amo,
tinto en la sangre del amo.

Sweat and the Lash

Lash,
sweat and the lash.

The sun was up early
and found the Black barefoot,
his scarred body naked,
in the field.

Lash,
sweat and the lash.

The wind went screaming by:
"Your hands are two black blossoms!"
His blood said to him: "Do it!"
He said to his blood: "I'll do it!"
He left, barefoot, in his blood.
The canefield, trembling,
let him pass.

Afterward, the silent sky,
and beneath the sky, the slave
stained with the master's blood.

Lash,
sweat and the lash,
stained with the master's blood.
Lash,
sweat and the lash,
stained with the master's blood,
stained with the master's blood.

El apellido

Elegía familiar

I

Desde la escuela
y aún antes . . . Desde el alba, cuando apenas
era una brizna yo de sueño y llanto,
desde entonces,
me dijeron mi nombre. Un santo y seña
para poder hablar con las estrellas.
Tú te llamas, te llamarás . . .
Y luego me entregaron
esto que veis escrito en mi tarjeta,
esto que pongo al pie de mis poemas:
las trece letras
que llevo a cuestas por la calle,
que siempre van conmigo a todas partes.
¿Es mi nombre, estáis ciertos?
¿Tenéis todas mis señas?
¿Ya conocéis mi sangre navegable,
mi geografía llena de oscuros montes,
de hondos y amargos valles
que no están en los mapas?
¿Acaso visitásteis mis abismos,
mis galerías subterráneas
con grandes piedras húmedas,
islas sobresaliendo en negras charcas
y donde un puro chorro
siento de antiguas aguas
caer desde mi alto corazón
con fresco y hondo estrépito

My Last Name

A family elegy

I

Ever since school
and even before . . . Since the dawn, when I was
barely a patch of sleep and wailing,
since then
I have been told my name. A password
that I might speak with stars.
Your name is, you shall be called . . .
And then they handed me
this you see here written on my card,
this I put at the foot of all my poems:
thirteen letters
that I carry on my shoulders through the street,
that are with me always, no matter where I go.
Are you sure it is my name?
Have you got all my particulars?
Do you already know my navigable blood,
my geography full of dark mountains,
of deep and bitter valleys
that are not on the maps?
Perhaps you have visited my chasms,
my subterranean galleries
with great moist rocks,
islands jutting out of black puddles,
where I feel the pure rush
of ancient waters
falling from my proud heart
with a sound that's fresh and deep

en un lugar lleno de ardientes árboles,
monos equilibristas,
loros legisladores y culebras?
¿Toda mi piel (debí decir)
toda mi piel viene de aquella estatua
de mármol español? ¿También mi voz de espanto,
el duro grito de mi garganta? ¿Vienen de allá
todos mis huesos? ¿Mis raíces y las raíces
de mis raíces y además
estas ramas oscuras movidas por los sueños
y estas flores abiertas en mi frente
y esta savia que amarga mi corteza?

¿Estáis seguros?
¿No hay nada más que eso que habéis escrito,
que eso que habéis sellado
con un sello de cólera?
(¡Oh, debí haber preguntado!)
Y bien, ahora os pregunto:
¿no veis estos tambores en mis ojos?
¿No veis estos tambores tensos y golpeados
con dos lágrimas secas?
¿No tengo acaso
un abuelo nocturno
con una gran marca negra
(más negra todavía que la piel)
una gran marca hecha de un latigazo?
¿No tengo pues
un abuelo mandinga, congo, dahomeyano?
¿Cómo se llama? ¡Oh, sí decídmelo!
¿Andrés? ¿Francisco? ¿Amable?
¿Cómo decís Andrés en congo?

to a place of flaming trees,
acrobatic monkeys,
legislative parrots and snakes?
Does all my skin (I should have said),
does all my skin come from that Spanish marble?
My frightening voice too,
the harsh cry in my throat?
Are all my bones from there?
My roots and the roots
of my roots and also
these dark branches swayed by dreams
and these flowers blooming on my forehead
and this sap embittering my bark?

Are you certain?
Is there nothing more than this that you have written,
than this which you have stamped
with the seal of anger?
(Oh, I should have asked!)
Well then, I ask you now:
Don't you see these drums in my eyes?
Don't you see these drums, tightened and
beaten with two dried-up tears?
Don't I have, perhaps,
a nocturnal grandfather
with a great black scar
(darker still than his skin)
a great scar made by a whip?
Have I not, then,
a grandfather who's Mandingo, Dahoman, Congolese?
What is his name? Oh, yes, give me his name!
Andrés? Francisco? Amable?
How do you say Andrés in Congolese?

¿Cómo habéis dicho siempre
Francisco en dahomeyano?
En mandinga ¿cómo se dice Amable?
¿O no? ¿Eran, pues, otros nombres?
¡El apellido, entonces!
¿Sabéis mi otro apellido, el que me viene
de aquella tierra enorme, el apellido
sangriento y capturado, que pasó sobre el mar
entre cadenas, que pasó entre cadenas sobre el mar?

¡Ah, no podéis recordarlo!
Lo habéis disuelto en tinta inmemorial.
Lo habéis robado a un pobre negro indefenso.
Lo escondisteis, creyendo
que iba a bajar los ojos yo de la vergüenza.
¡Gracias!
¡Os lo agradezco!
¡Gentiles gentes, thank you!
Merci!
Merci bien!
Merci beaucoup!
Pero no . . . ¿Podéis creerlo? No.
Yo estoy limpio.
Brilla mi voz como un metal recién pulido.
Mirad mi escudo: tiene un baobad,
tiene un rinoceronte y una lanza.
Yo soy también el nieto,
biznieto,
tataranieto de un esclavo.
(Que se avergüence el amo.)
¿Seré Yelofe?
¿Nicolás Yelofe, acaso?
¿O Nicolás Bakongo?

164

How have you always said
Francisco in Dahoman?
In Mandingo, how do you say Amable?
No? Were they, then, other names?
The last name then!
Do you know my other last name, the one that comes
to me from that enormous land, the captured,
bloody last name, that came across the sea
in chains, which came in chains across the sea?

Ah, you can't remember it!
You have dissolved it in immemorial ink.
You stole it from a poor, defenseless Black.
You hid it, thinking that I would
lower my eyes in shame.
Thank you!
I am grateful to you!
Noble people, thanks!
Merci!
Merci bien!
Merci beaucoup!
But no . . . Can you believe it? No.
I am clean.
My voice sparkles like newly polished metal.
Look at my shield: it has a baobab,
it has a rhinoceros and a spear.
I am also the grandson,
great grandson,
great great grandson of a slave.
(Let the master be ashamed.)
Am I Yelofe?
Nicolás Yelofe, perhaps?
Or Nicolás Bakongo?

¿Tal vez Guillén Banguila?
¿O Kumbá?
¿Quizá Guillén Kumbá?
¿O Kongué?
¿Pudiera ser Guillén Kongué?
¡Oh, quién lo sabe!
¡Qué enigma entre las aguas!

II

Siento la noche inmensa gravitar
sobre profundas bestias,
sobre inocentes almas castigadas;
pero también sobre voces en punta,
que despojan al cielo de sus soles,
los más duros,
para condecorar la sangre combatiente.
De algún país ardiente, perforado
por la gran flecha ecuatorial,
sé que vendrán lejanos primos,
remota angustia mía disparada en el viento;
sé que vendrán pedazos de mis venas,
sangre remota mía,
con duro pie aplastando las hierbas asustadas;
sé que vendrán hombres de vidas verdes,
remota selva mía,
con su dolor abierto en cruz y el pecho rojo en llamas.

Sin conocernos nos reconoceremos en el hambre,
en la tuberculosis y en la sífilis,
en el sudor comprado en bolsa negra,
en los fragmentos de cadenas
adheridos todavía a la piel;

Maybe Guillén Banguila?
Or Kumbá?
Perhaps Guillén Kumbá?
Or Kongué?
Could I be Guillén Kongué?
Oh, who knows!
What a riddle in the waters!

II

I feel immense night fall
on profound beasts,
on innocent castigated souls;
but also on ready voices,
which steal suns from the sky,
the brightest suns,
to decorate combatant blood.
From some flaming land pierced through
by the great equatorial arrow,
I know there will come distant cousins,
my ancestral anguish cast upon the winds;
I know there will come portions of my veins,
my ancestral blood,
with calloused feet bending frightened grasses;
I know there will come men whose lives are green,
my ancestral jungle,
with their pain open like a cross and their breasts red with
    flames.

Having never met, we will know each other by the hunger,
by the tuberculosis and the syphilis,
by the sweat bought in a black market,
by the fragments of chain
still clinging to the skin;

sin conocernos nos reconoceremos
en los ojos cargados de sueños
y hasta en los insultos como piedras
que nos escupen cada día
los cuadrumanos de la tinta y el papel.
¿Qué ha de importar entonces
(¡qué ha de importar ahora!)
¡ay! mi pequeño nombre
de trece letras blancas?
¿Ni el mandinga, bantú,
yoruba, dahomeyano
nombre del triste abuelo ahogado
en tinta de notario?
¿Qué importa, amigos puros?
¡Oh sí, puros amigos,
venid a ver mi nombre!
Mi nombre interminable,
hecho de interminables nombres;
el nombre mío, ajeno,
libre y mío, ajeno y vuestro,
ajeno y libre como el aire.

having never met we will know each other
by the dream-full eyes
and even by the rock-hard insults
the quadrumanes of ink and paper
spit at us each day.
What can it matter, then?
(What does it matter now!)
Ah, my little name
of thirteen letters?
Or the Mandingo, Bantu,
Yoruba, Dahoman name
of the sad grandfather drowned
in notary's ink.
Good friends, what does it matter?
Oh, yes, good friends
come look at my name!
My name without end,
made up of endless names;
my name, foreign,
free and mine, foreign and yours,
foreign and free as the air.

Canción puertorriqueña

¿Cómo estás, Puerto Rico,
tú de socio asociado en sociedad?
Al pie de cocoteros y guitarras,
bajo la luna y junto al mar,
¡qué suave honor andar del brazo,
brazo con brazo, del Tío Sam!
¿En qué lengua me entiendes,
en qué lengua por fin te podré hablar,
si en yes,
si en sí,
si en bien,
si en well,
si en mal,
si en bad, si en very bad?

Juran los que te matan
que eres feliz . . . ¿Será verdad?
Arde tu frente pálida,
la anemia en tu mirada logra un brillo fatal;
masticas una jerigonza
medio española, medio slang;
de un empujón te hundieron en Corea,
sin que supieras por quién ibas a pelear,
si en yes,
si en sí,
si en bien,
si en well,
si en mal,
si en bad, si en very bad!

Puerto Rican Song

How are you, Puerto Rico,
associate associated in society?
At the foot of coco-palms and guitars,
under the moon, by the sea,
what a sweet honor to walk,
arm in arm, with Uncle Sam!
In what language do you understand me,
in what tongue, in short, shall I speak to you;
in yes,
in sí
in bien,
in well,
in mal,
in bad, in very bad?

Those who are killing you swear
that you are content . . . Is it true?
Your pale forehead burns,
the anemia in your glance gives off a fatal brilliance;
you chew a jargon
half-Spanish, half-slang;
they sank you with a shove into Korea,
without knowing for whom you were going to fight,
or if in yes,
in sí,
in bien,
in well,
in mal,
in bad, in very bad!

Ay, yo bien conozco a tu enemigo,
el mismo que tenemos por acá,
socio en la sangre y el azúcar,
socio asociado en sociedad:
United States and Puerto Rico,
es decir New York City with San Juan,
Manhattan y Borinquen, soga y cuello,
apenas nada más . . .
No yes,
no sí,
no bien,
no well,
sí mal,
sí bad, sí very bad.

Oh, how well I know your enemy,
the same one we have here,
a partner in our blood and our sugar,
associate associated in society:
the United States and Puerto Rico,
that is, New York City with San Juan,
Manhattan and Borinquen, noose and neck;
hardly anything else . . .
Not yes,
Not sí,
Not bien,
Not well,
but mal,
yes bad, yes very bad!

Line 2: a reference to the colonial status of Puerto Rico. Taken from Spain by conquest in 1898, the island was declared a Commonwealth by an act of the U.S. Congress on July 25, 1952, when, in the jargon of the empire, it became "a free associate state" of the United States.

Line 7, last stanza: Borinquen is the original Indian name for Puerto Rico, and is commonly used when referring to the island.

Está bien

Está muy bien que cantes cuando lloras, negro hermano,
negro del Sur crucificado;
bien tus *spirituals*,
tus estandartes,
tus marchas, y los alegatos
de tus abogados.
Está muy bien.

Bien que patines en pos de la justicia,
—¡oh aquel ingenuo patinador
tragando aire hasta Washington desde Chicago!—
bien tus protestas en los diarios,
bien tus puños cerrados
y Lincoln en su retrato.
Está muy bien.

Bien tus sermones en los templos dinamitados,
bien tu insistencia heroica
en estar junto a los blancos,
porque la ley—¿la ley?—proclama
la igualdad de todos los americanos.
             Bien.
             Está muy bien.
             Requetebién,
hermano negro del Sur crucificado.
Pero acuérdate de John Brown,
que no era negro y te defendió con un fusil en las manos.

Fusil: arma de fuego portátil
(es lo que dice el diccionario)

174

It is all very well

It is all very well that you sing as you weep, brother Black,
Black man of the crucified South;
Your spirituals are fine,
your banners,
your marches, and the allegations
of your legal counsel.
It is all very well.

Well that you skate in search of justice
(oh that ingenuous skater
swallowing air into Washington from Chicago!),
well your protests in the daily papers,
well your clenched fists and
Lincoln in his portrait.
It is all very well.

Well your sermons in dynamited temples,
well your heroic insistence on
being together with the white,
for the law—the law?—proclaims
the equality of all Americans.
       Well.
       It is all well.
       It is all very well,
Black brother of the crucified South.
But don't forget John Brown,
who was not Black and who defended you *fusil* in hand.

Fusil: a portable firearm
(it's what the dictionary says)

con que disparan los soldados.
Hay que agregar: Fusil (en inglés "gun"):
arma también con que responden
los esclavos.

Pero si ocurre (eso acontece),
pero si ocurre, hermano,
que no tienes fusil, pues entonces
en ese caso,
digo, no sé,
búscate algo
—una mandarria, un palo,
una piedra—algo
que duela,
algo duro que hiera,
que golpée,
que saque sangre,
algo.

with which the soldiers shoot.
One has to add: *Fusil* (in English "gun"):
a weapon also
with which the slaves respond.

But if it happens (that does occur),
but if it happens, brother,
that you have no gun,
well then, in that case,
I say, I don't know,
find yourself something—
a sledgehammer, a stick,
a rock—something
that will hurt,
something hard that will wound,
that will bruise,
which will draw blood,
something.

Soldados en Abisinia

Mussolini.
Sobre el puño, la barba.
Sobre la mesa, en cruz,
Africa
desangrada.
Africa verdinegra y azulblanca,
de geografía y mapa.

El dedo, hijo de César,
penetra el continente:
no hablan las aguas de papel,
ni los desiertos de papel,
ni las ciudades de papel.
El mapa, frío, de papel,
y el dedo, hijo de César,
con la uña sangrienta, ya clavada,
sobre una Abisinia de papel.

¡Qué diablo de pirata,
Mussolini,
con la cara tan dura
y la mano tan larga!
Abisinia se encrespa,
se enarca,
grita,
rabia,
protesta.
¡Il Duce!
Soldados.

Soldiers in Abyssinia

Mussolini.
On his fist, his beard.
On the table, like a cross,
Africa
bleeding.
Greenish-black and bluish-white Africa
of geography and the map.

His finger, son of Caesar,
pierces the continent:
the paper waters
do not speak,
nor do the paper deserts,
nor do the cities of paper.
The map, impassive, is paper,
and his finger, son of Caesar,
with its bloody nail, is fixed
on a paper Abyssinia.

What a diabolical pirate,
Mussolini,
with so hard a face
and so long a hand!
Abyssinia bristles,
arches itself,
screams,
rages,
protests.
Il Duce!
Soldiers.

Guerra.
Barcos.

Mussolini, en automóvil,
da su paseo matinal;
Mussolini, a caballo,
en su ejercicio vesperal;
Mussolini, en avión,
de una ciudad a otra ciudad.
Mussolini, bañado,
fresco,
limpio,
vertiginoso.
Mussolini, contento.
Y serio.

¡Ah, pero los soldados
irán cayendo y tropezando!
Los soldados
no harán su viaje sobre un mapa,
sino sobre el suelo de Africa,
bajo el sol de Africa.
Allá no encontrarán ciudades de papel;
las ciudades serán algo más que puntos que hablen
con verdes vocecitas topográficas:
hormigueros de balas,
toses de ametralladoras,
cañaverales de lanzas.
Entonces, los soldados,
(que no hicieron su viaje sobre un mapa)
los soldados,
lejos de Mussolini,
solos;

War.
Ships.

Mussolini, in a car,
goes for his morning drive;
Mussolini, on horseback,
during his evening exercise;
Mussolini, by airplane,
from one city to another.
Mussolini, bathed,
fresh,
clean,
capricious.
Mussolini, content.
And serious.

Ah, but the soldiers
will fall and stumble!
The soldiers
will not travel on a map,
but on the ground of Africa,
under Africa's sun.
There they will not find paper cities;
the cities will be something more than dots that speak
with little green topographical voices:
a swarm of bullets,
submachine-gun coughs,
canefields of lances.
Then, the soldiers,
(who did not travel on a map),
the soldiers,
far from Mussolini,
alone;

los soldados
se abrasarán en el desierto,
y mucho más pequeños, desde luego,
los soldados
irán secándose después lentamente al sol
los soldados
devueltos,
los soldados
en el excremento de los buitres.

the soldiers
will roast in the desert,
and much smaller, of course,
the soldiers
will then slowly dry up in the sun
the soldiers
come back,
the soldiers
in the excrement of buzzards.

183

WAYNESBURG COLLEGE LIBRARY
WAYNESBURG, PA.

No sé por qué piensas tú

No sé por qué piensas tú,
soldado, que te odio yo,
si somos la misma cosa
yo,
tú.

Tú eres pobre, lo soy yo;
soy de abajo, lo eres tú;
¿de dónde has sacado tú,
soldado, que te odio yo?

Me duele que a veces tú
te olvides de quién soy yo;
caramba, si yo soy tú,
lo mismo que tú eres yo.

Pero no por eso yo
he de malquererte, tú;
si somos la misma cosa,
yo,
tú,
no sé por qué piensas tú,
soldado, que te odio yo.

Ya nos veremos yo y tú,
juntos en la misma calle,
hombro con hombro, tú y yo,
sin odios ni yo ni tú,
pero sabiendo tú y yo,
a dónde vamos yo y tú . . .
¡No sé por qué piensas tú,
soldado, que te odio yo!

Why, soldier, does it seem to you

Why, soldier, does it seem to you
that hatred is lurking in me,
if we're exactly the same,
me,
you.

You are poor; just look at me.
I come from below, so do you:
How did it occur to you,
soldier, that hatred is within me?

It hurts me at times that you
tend to forget I am me;
caramba, since I am you,
the same way that you are me.

But, despite what you think of me,
I'll bear no malice toward you;
if we're exactly the same,
me,
you,
why, soldier, does it seem to you
that hatred is lurking in me.

We'll soon see each other, me and you,
walking together in the street,
shoulder to shoulder, you and me,
without hatred, me or you,
but knowing for certain, you and me,
where we are going, me and you . . .
Why, soldier, does it seem to you
that hatred is lurking in me!

¿Puedes?

a Lumir Civrny, en Praga

¿Puedes venderme el aire que pasa entre tus dedos
y te golpea la cara y te despeina?
¿Tal vez podrías venderme cinco pesos de viento,
o más, quizás venderme una tormenta?
¿Acaso el aire fino
me venderías, el aire
(no todo) que recorre
en tu jardín corolas y corolas,
en tu jardín para los pájaros,
diez pesos de aire fino?

    El aire gira y pasa
    en una mariposa.
    Nadie lo tiene, nadie.

¿Puedes venderme cielo,
el cielo azul a veces,
o gris también a veces,
una parcela de tu cielo,
el que compraste, piensas tú, con los árboles
de tu huerto, como quien compra el techo con la casa?
¿Puedes venderme un dólar
de cielo, dos kilómetros
de cielo, un trozo, el que tú puedas,
de tu cielo?

    El cielo está en las nubes.
    Altas las nubes pasan.
    Nadie las tiene, nadie.

Can You?

for Lumir Civrny, in Prague

Can you sell me the air that passes through your fingers
and hits your face and undoes your hair?
Maybe you could sell me five dollars' worth of wind,
or more, perhaps sell me a cyclone?
Maybe you would sell me
the thin air, the air
(not all of it) that sweeps
into your garden blossom on blossom
into your garden for the birds,
ten dollars of pure air.

     The air it turns and passes
     with butterfly-like spins.
     No one owns it, no one.

Can you sell me some sky,
the sky that's blue at times,
or gray again at times,
a small part of your sky,
the one you bought—you think—with all the trees
of your orchard, as one who buys the ceiling with the
    house?
Can you sell me a dollar's worth
of sky, two miles
of sky, a fragment of your sky,
whatever piece you can?

     The sky is in the clouds.
     The clouds are high, they pass.
     No one owns them, no one.

¿Puedes venderme lluvia, el agua
que te ha dado tus lágrimas y te moja la lengua?
¿Puedes venderme un dólar de agua
de manantial, una nube preñada,
crespa y suave como una cordera,
o bien agua llovida en la montaña,
o el agua de los charcos
abandonados a los perros,
o una legua de mar, tal vez un lago,
cien dólares de lago?

   El agua cae, rueda.
   El agua rueda, pasa.
   Nadie la tiene, nadie.

¿Puedes venderme tierra, la profunda
noche de las raíces, dientes
de dinosaurios y la cal
dispersa de lejanos esqueletos?
¿Puedes venderme selvas ya sepultadas, aves muertas,
peces de piedra, azufre
de los volcanes, mil millones de años
en espiral subiendo? ¿Puedes
venderme tierra, puedes
venderme tierra, puedes?

   La tierra tuya es mía
   todos los pies la pisan.
   Nadie la tiene, nadie.

Can you sell me some rain, the water
that has given you your tears and wets your tongue?
Can you sell me a dollar's worth of water
from the spring, a pregnant cloud,
as soft and graceful as a lamb,
or even water fallen on the mountain,
or water gathered in the ponds
abandoned to the dogs,
or one league of the sea, a lake perhaps,
a hundred dollars' worth of lake?

> The water falls, it runs.
> The water runs, it passes.
> No one holds it, no one.

Can you sell me some land, the deep night
of the roots, the teeth of
dinosaurs and the scattered lime
of distant skeletons?
Can you sell me long since buried jungles, birds now ex-
    tinct,
fish fossilized, the sulphur
of volcanoes, a thousand million years
rising in spiral? Can you
sell me some land, can you
sell me some land, can you?

> The land that's yours is mine.
> The feet of all walk on it.
> No one owns it, no one.

Tengo

Cuando me veo y toco
yo, Juan sin Nada no más ayer,
y hoy Juan con Todo,
y hoy con todo,
vuelvo los ojos, miro,
me veo y toco
y me pregunto cómo ha podido ser.

Tengo, vamos a ver,
tengo el gusto de andar por mi país,
dueño de cuanto hay en él,
mirando bien de cerca lo que antes
no tuve ni podía tener.
Zafra puedo decir,
monte puedo decir,
ciudad puedo decir,
ejército decir,
ya míos para siempre y tuyos, nuestros,
y un ancho resplandor
de rayo, estrella, flor.

Tengo, vamos a ver,
tengo el gusto de ir
yo, campesino, obrero, gente simple,
tengo el gusto de ir
(es un ejemplo)
a un banco y hablar con el administrador,
no en inglés,
no en señor,
sino decirle compañero como se dice en español.

I have

When I look at and touch myself,
I, John-only-yesterday-with-Nothing,
and John-with-Everything-today,
with everything today,
I glance around, I look and see
and touch myself and wonder
how it could have happened.

I have, let's see:
I have the pleasure of walking my country,
the owner of all there is in it,
examining at very close range what
I could not and did not have before.
I can say cane,
I can say mountain,
I can say city,
I can say army,
army say,
now mine forever and yours, ours,
and the vast splendor of
the sunbeam, the star, the flower.

I have, let's see:
I have the pleasure of going,
me, a peasant, a worker, a simple man,
I have the pleasure of going
(just an example)
to a bank and speaking to the manager,
not in English,
not in "Sir,"
but in *compañero* as we say in Spanish.

Tengo, vamos a ver,
que siendo un negro
nadie me puede detener
a la puerta de un dancing o de un bar.
O bien en la carpeta de un hotel
gritarme que no hay pieza,
una mínima pieza y no una pieza colosal,
una pequeña pieza donde yo pueda descansar.

Tengo, vamos a ver,
que no hay guardia rural
que me agarre y me encierre en un cuartel,
ni me arranque y me arroje de mi tierra
al medio del camino real.

Tengo que como tengo la tierra tengo el mar,
no country, no jailáif,
no tennis y no yacht,
sino de playa en playa y ola en ola,
gigante azul abierto democrático:
en fin, el mar.

Tengo, vamos a ver,
que ya aprendí a leer,
a contar,
tengo que ya aprendí a escribir
y a pensar
y a reír.
Tengo que ya tengo
donde trabajar
y ganar

I have, let's see:
that being Black
I can be stopped by no one at
the door of a dancing hall or bar.
Or even at the desk of a hotel
have someone yell at me there are no rooms,
a small room and not one that's immense,
a tiny room where I might rest.

I have, let's see:
that there are no rural police
to seize me and lock me in a precinct jail,
or tear me from my land and cast me
in the middle of the highway.

I have that having the land I have the sea,
no country clubs,
no high life,
no tennis and no yachts,
but, from beach to beach and wave on wave,
gigantic blue open democratic:
in short, the sea.

I have, let's see:
that I have learned to read,
to count,
I have that I have learned to write,
and to think
and to laugh.
I have that now I have
a place to work
and earn

lo que me tengo que comer.
Tengo, vamos a ver,
tengo lo que tenía que tener.

what I have to eat.
I have, let's see:
I have what was coming to me.

This version was originally published in *Antología mayor*. The final version, published in the book to which the poem gives title (*Tengo*, 1967), omits the fourth line of the first stanza.

Responde tú . . .

Tú, que partiste de Cuba,
responde tú,
¿dónde hallarás verde y verde,
azul y azul,
palma y palma bajo el cielo?
Responde tú.

Tú, que tu lengua olvidaste,
responde tú,
y en lengua extraña masticas
el güel y el yu,
¿cómo vivir puedes mudo?
Responde tú.

Tú, que dejaste la tierra,
responde tú,
donde tu padre reposa
bajo una cruz,
¿dónde dejarás tus huesos?
Responde tú.

Ah, desdichado, responde,
responde tú,
¿dónde hallarás verde y verde,
azul y azul,
palma y palma bajo el cielo?
Responde tú.

Tell me . . .

You, who went out of Cuba,
tell me,
where will you find green after green,
blue after blue,
palm after palm under the sky?
Tell me.

You, who have forgotten your language,
tell me,
and chew in an alien tongue
the *guël* and the *yu*,
how can you live in silence?
Tell me.

You, who left behind the land,
tell me,
where your father lies
beneath a cross,
where will you leave your bones?
Tell me.

Oh, poor wretch, answer,
tell me,
where will you find green after green,
blue after blue,
palm after palm under the sky?
Tell me.

La herencia

Al fin te marchas, claro. Muy bien. Eso no es nada.
Si acaso, el momentáneo desempleo,
la granja;
tal vez, como perro temeroso,
los ojos bajos un instante, al pasar
frente a aquel compañero que te creía otra cosa.
Y de repente, Miami. Como si dijéramos La Habana
que buscabas,
tu Habana fácil y despreocupada.
(Políticos baratos ¡que costaban tan caro!
Burdeles, juego, yanquis, mariguana.)
Magnífico.
Un salto atrás perfecto.
Eres un gran prospecto
olímpico.

Sin embargo, no sé qué penetrante
qué desasosegada
lástima me aprieta el corazón, pensando
en tus remotos descendientes,
dormidos en su gran noche previa,
su gran noche nonata.

Porque algún día imprevisible,
aún no establecido, pero cierto,
van a verse acosados
por la pregunta necesaria.
Tal vez en la clase de historia
algún camarada.
Acaso en una fábrica. La novia

The Inheritance

You are finally leaving, naturally. Fine. That's all right.
Maybe it was the momentary unemployment,
the farm;
perhaps it was passing, eyes lowered
for an instant, a timid dog,
before the friend who thought you something better.
Then suddenly, Miami. As if to say Havana,
the Havana you were looking for,
your easy, unprepossessing Havana.
(Cheap politicians who were so expensive!
Brothels, gambling, Yankees, marijuana.)
Magnificent.
A perfect leap backward.
You are a great
Olympic prospect.

And yet, I do not know what piercing,
what disquieting
grief clutches at my heart, when I think
about your still remote descendants,
sleeping in their great antecedent night,
their immense nothingness night.

For some unforeseen day,
not yet established, but certain,
they will see themselves tormented
by the inevitable question.
It may be a schoolmate
in a history class.
Perhaps in a factory. It might be

pudiera ser. En cualquier sitio, en fin,
donde se hable de este hoy
que será para entonces un portentoso ayer.
Sabrán lo que es la herencia que les dejas,
esta especie de sífilis
que ahora testas con tu fuga,
algo así como aquella otra sífilis (verdadera)
que denuncia tu labio leporino,
y que ganó tu abuelo,
contrabandista, marinero,
bandido,
cierta noche de escándalo
bajo la luna de los caribes,
borracho con una horrenda puta
en Cartagena o Panamá.

Claro que sé muy bien
lo que hay que responder en estos casos.
(Que los hijos no pagan la cuenta de los padres,
que los padres, etcétera.)
De acuerdo,
mas con todo, no es lo mismo.
Uno se siente más tranquilo
con Maceo allá arriba,
ardiendo en el gran sol de nuestra sangre,
que con Weyler vertiéndola a sablazos.
Cuestión de suerte, me dirás. ¿No es eso?
Quizás, te diré yo. Pero así es.

a girlfriend. Anywhere, in short,
where they speak of this today
which will then be a prodigious yesterday.
They will realize what inheritance you leave them,
this species of syphilis
you bequeath with your escape,
something like that other (real) syphilis
announced by your harelip
and won by your grandfather,
a smuggler, sailor, bandit,
a certain scandalous night,
drunk with an ugly whore
in Cartagena or Panama.

Of course I know very well
what one has to answer in cases like this.
(That the sons do not pay for the sins of the fathers,
that the fathers, etcetera.)
Agreed,
but with all that, still it's not the same.
One feels more at ease
with Maceo up there,
burning in the great sun of our blood,
than with Weyler spilling it by sword.
A matter of luck, you will say. Isn't that it?
Perhaps, I will answer. But that's the way it is.

Line 8, fourth stanza: Antonio Maceo Grajales (1845–1896) is a
Cuban national hero, a Black, and with Martí one of the leading figures
in the Revolution of 1895.

Line 10, fifth stanza: General Valeriano Weyler was commander of
Spanish forces during the Cuban revolutionary war of 1895. He fol-
lowed a policy of complete ruthlessness during his campaign and is par-
ticularly remembered for his policy of moving the Cuban population
into compounds, reconcentrados, in order to prevent their helping the
rebel forces.

201

Problemas del subdesarrollo

Monsieur Dupont te llama inculto,
porque ignoras cuál era el nieto
preferido de Víctor Hugo.

Herr Müller se ha puesto a gritar,
porque no sabes el día
(exacto) que murió Bismarck.

Mr. Smith,
inglés o yanqui, yo no lo sé,
se subleva cuando escribes *shell*.
(Parece que ahorras una ele,
y que además pronuncias *chel*.)

Bueno ¿y qué?
Cuando te toque a ti,
mándales decir Huancavelica,
y que dónde está el Aconcagua,
y que quién era Sucre,
y que en qué lugar de este planeta
murió Martí.
(Por favor:
que te hablen siempre en español.)

Problems of Underdevelopment

Monsieur Dupont calls you uncultured
because you cannot say who was
Victor Hugo's favorite grandson.

Herr Müller has started to scream
because you do not know (exactly)
the day that Bismarck died.

Mr. Smith,
an Englishman or Yankee, I cannot tell,
explodes when you write *Shell.*
(It seems that you eliminate an *l*
and, what is more, pronounce it *chel.*)

Well, so what?
When your turn comes,
tell them to say Huancavelica,
and where the Aconcagua's found,
and who was Sucre,
and in what spot on the planet
Martí died.
(Please:
have them always speak to you in Spanish.)

Line 14: Huancavelica is a town in the Peruvian Andes.
Line 16: Antonio José de Sucre (1793–1830) was a Venezuelan general, one of the liberators of South America and first president of Bolivia.

Proposiciones para explicar la muerte de Ana

Ana murió de un tiro en el estómago.
Ana murió de un tiro en su retrato.
Ana murió de dos y dos son cuatro.
Ana murió de un solo brazo.

Ana murió de tisis y de hongos.
Ana murió de un vuelo de comandos.
Ana murió de hipo y de catarro.
Ana murió de un venenazo.

Ana murió de su langosta enferma.
Ana murió de huevos y arroz blanco.
Ana murió de azufre y arseniato.

Ana murió de hallarse sin socorro.
Ana murió de un mal nada romántico.
Ana murió de un sifilazo.

Propositions on the Death of Ana

Ana died from a shot in the stomach.
Ana died from a bullet lodged in her portrait.
Ana died from two plus two are four.
Ana died from a single arm.

Ana died from consumption and mushrooms.
Ana died from a commando air raid.
Ana died from hiccups and a cold.
Ana died from being given poison.

Ana died from eating her sick lobster.
Ana died from eggs and white rice.
Ana died from sulphur and arsenate.

Ana died from finding herself without hope.
Ana died from a sickness not at all romantic.
Ana died from a syphilitic wound.

This is an original manuscript version of the poem.

Papier peint

La señora cajera me lo dijo:
Salga usted de sus dólares.
En todo caso, compre
lingotes de oro. Acciones
del Transvaal (las minas de diamantes).
Desembuche, defeque
todos sus travels.
Dentro de pocos meses
vera usted los sangrientos
certificados de papel
hechos papel para forrar paredes.
Papel vuelto papel.

Es lo que dice el cable.
Es lo que vociferan susurrando
los pasajeros de primera
en puertos y aeropuertos;
lo que las gentes cuentan con pavor,
como si huyeran
de la caída de un gobierno
y los incendios y motines que suelen venir luego.

Está bien. Si lo dijo
la señora cajera, será cierto.
De modo pues que cuando
el gran balón estalle,
cuando la cosa llegue
(fantástico si fuera en estas Pascuas)
podré tapar alegremente
con retratos McKinley repetidos en cada vez

Papier Peint

The lady cashier told me:
get rid of all your dollars.
In any case, buy gold
ingots. Invest
in the Transvaal (diamond mines).
Throw up, defecate
your travelers checks.
In a few months
you will see the blood-stained
paper certificates
turn into paper for decorating walls.
Paper turned to paper.

That is what the cable says.
It's what first-class passengers,
whispering, vociferate
in piers and airports,
what people say in fear,
as if fleeing
from the downfall of a government
and from the burning and the riots that usually come
     after.

Fine. If the cashier
said it, it must be true.
So that when the great balloon explodes,
when the thing does come
(how fantastic if it were this Christmas)
I can cheerfully cover up
with pictures of McKinley duplicated

207

quinientos dólares
un lienzo desconchado y melancólico que hay
en mi sombrío water closet;
con Hamilton diez dólares
y Hamilton y Hamilton
esconder cocodrilos, peces, dinosaurios,
toda una fauna cuaternaria
que ha dibujado la humedad
en el panel izquierdo de mi estudio;
el bueno de Abraham barbas de cinco dólares
me ayudará en la biblioteca (empapelarla);
la cabeza ceniza veinte dólares ladrón
de Texas Mr. Jackson,
veremos como irá (puede que en la cocina);
y donde quiera
que haya lugar, Washington el Jorge se ha de ver
serio, casi dramático, como cuadra al patrón.

Nunca siendo tan pobre
habré gastado tanto.
Más de un millón de dólares.
Qué emoción.

on each five hundred dollar bill
a peeling, melancholic stretch of wall
in my sombre water closet;
with Hamilton ten dollars
and Hamilton and Hamilton
hide crocodiles, fish, dinosaurs,
a whole Quaternary fauna
drawn by the humidity
on the left side panel of my study;
honest Abraham with a five-dollar beard
will be of help in (wall-papering) the library;
the gray-headed twenty dollar thief
from Texas, Mr. Jackson,
we'll see how he goes
(in the kitchen perhaps)
and wherever
there is any room, Washington, George, will be seen
grave, almost dramatic, as befits the master.

Being so poor, I never
will have spent so much.
More than a million dollars.
How exciting.

Digo que yo no soy un hombre puro

Yo no voy a decirte que soy un hombre puro.
Entre otras cosas
falta saber si es que lo puro existe.
O si es, pongamos, necesario.
O posible.
O si sabe bien.
¿Acaso has tú probado el agua químicamente pura,
el agua de laboratorio,
sin un grano de tierra o de estiércol,
sin el pequeño excremento de un pájaro,
el agua hecha no más que de oxígeno e hidrógeno?
¡Puah! qué porquería.

Yo no te digo pues que soy un hombre puro,
yo no te digo eso, sino todo lo contrario.
Que amo (a las mujeres, naturalmente,
pues mi amor puede decir su nombre),
y me gusta comer carne de puerco con papas,
y garbanzos y chorizos, y
huevos, pollos, carneros, pavos,
pescados y mariscos,
y bebo ron y cerveza y aguardiente y vino,
y fornico (incluso con el estómago lleno).
Soy impuro ¿qué quieres que te diga?
Completamente impuro.

Sin embargo,
creo que hay muchas cosas puras en el mundo
que no son más que pura mierda.
Por ejemplo, la pureza del virgo nonagenario.

I Declare Myself an Impure Man

I am not going to tell you that I am a pure man.
Among other things
we have yet to know if what is pure exists.
Or if it is, say, necessary.
Or possible.
Or if it tastes good.
Have you ever had chemically pure water,
laboratory water,
without a grain of dirt or excrement,
without a bird's small excrement,
water composed only of oxygen and hydrogen?
Puah! What filth!

I do not say, then, that I am a pure man,
I will not tell you that: everything to the contrary.
That I love (women, naturally,
for my love can speak its name),
and like to eat pork with potatoes,
and chickpeas and sausages, and
eggs, chicken, lamb, turkey,
fish and clams;
and I drink rum and beer and brandy and wine,
and fornicate (even on a full stomach).
I am impure, what can I say?
Absolutely impure.

But,
I think there are many pure things in the world
that are nothing but pure shit.
For example, the purity of a ninety-year-old hymen.

211

La pureza de los novios que se masturban
en vez de acostarse juntos en una posada.
La pureza de los colegios de internado, donde
abre sus flores de semen provisional
la fauna pederasta.
La pureza de los clérigos.
La pureza de los académicos.
La pureza de los gramáticos.
La pureza de los que aseguran
que hay que.ser puros, puros, puros.
La pureza de los que nunca tuvieron blenorragia.
La pureza de la mujer que nunca lamió un glande.
La pureza del hombre que nunca succionó un clítoris.
La pureza de la que nunca parió.
La pureza del que no engendró nunca.
La pureza del que se da golpes en el pecho, y
dice santo, santo, santo,
cuando es un diablo, diablo, diablo.
En fin, la pureza
de quien no llegó a ser lo suficientemente impuro
para saber qué cosa es la pureza.

Punto, fecha y firma.
Así lo dejo escrito.

The purity of lovers who masturbate
instead of going to bed together in some inn.
The purity of boarding schools
where a pederastic fauna
opens its blossoms of provisional semen.
The purity of the clergy.
The purity of the academics.
The purity of the grammarians.
The purity of those who assure us
that we must be pure, pure, pure.
The purity of those who never had blennorrhoea.
The purity of the woman who never licked a glans.
The purity of the man who never sucked on a clitoris.
The purity of the woman who never gave birth.
The purity of the man who never laid a seed.
The purity of the man who beats his breast
and says saint, saint, saint,
when he is a devil, devil, devil.
In short, the purity
of anyone who never was sufficiently impure
to know what purity is.

Period, date, and signature.
So I leave it written.

Che Comandante

No porque hayas caído
tu luz es menos alta.
Un caballo de fuego
sostiene tu escultura guerrillera
entre el viento y las nubes de la Sierra.
No por callado eres silencio.
Y no porque te quemen,
porque te disimulen bajo tierra,
porque te escondan
en cementerios, bosques, páramos,
van a impedir que te encontremos,
Che Comandante,
amigo.

Con sus dientes de júbilo
Norteamérica ríe. Mas de pronto
revuélvese en su lecho
de dólares. Se le cuaja
la risa en una máscara,
y tu gran cuerpo de metal
sube, se disemina
en las guerrillas como tábanos,
y tu ancho nombre herido por soldados
ilumina la noche americana
como una estrella súbita, caída
en medio de una orgía.
Tú lo sabías, Guevara,
pero no lo dijiste por modestia,
por no hablar de ti mismo,
Che Comandante,
amigo.

Che Comandante

Not because you have fallen
is your light less high.
A horse of fire
sustains you, guerrilla sculpture,
between the wind and the clouds of the Sierra.
Not because you are mute are you silence.
And not because they burn you,
not because they hide you in the earth,
conceal you in cemeteries,
forests, bleak plateaus,
will they prevent our finding you,
Che Comandante,
friend.

North America laughs
with its teeth of joy. But suddenly
it turns over in its bed
of dollars. The laugh
solidifies into a mask
and your great metal body
rises, spreads itself among
the gadfly-like guerrilla bands,
and your wide soldier-wounded name
illuminates the American night
like a star fallen suddenly
in the midst of an orgy.
You knew it, Guevara,
but would not say so out of modesty,
in order not to speak about yourself,
Che Comandante,
friend.

Estás en todas partes. En el indio
hecho de sueño y cobre. Y en el negro
revuelto en espumosa muchedumbre,
y en el ser petrolero y salitrero,
y en el terrible desamparo
de la banana, y en la gran pampa de las pieles,
y en el azúcar y en la sal y en los cafetos,
tú, móvil estatua de tu sangre como te derribaron,
vivo, como no te querían,
Che Comandante,
amigo.

Cuba te sabe de memoria. Rostro
de barbas que clarean. Y marfil
y aceituna en la piel de santo joven.
Firme la voz que ordena sin mandar,
que manda compañera, ordena amiga,
tierna y dura de jefe camarada.
Te vemos cada día ministro,
cada día soldado, cada día
gente llana y difícil
cada día.
Y puro como un niño
o como un hombre puro,
Che Comandante,
amigo.

Pasas en tu descolorido, roto, agujereado
traje de campaña.
El de la selva, como antes

You are everywhere. In the Indian made
of drowsiness and copper. And in the Black
lost in a foamy multitude;
in the oil worker, in the nitrate worker,
and in the terrible abandonment
of the banana; in the great plains of the hides,
in the sugar, in the salt, and in the coffee trees,
you, a mobile statue of your blood as you had fallen;
alive, as they did not want you,
Che Comandante,
friend.

Cuba knows you by heart. A face
with a transparent beard. Ivory
and olive in the skin of a young saint.
A firm voice that orders without commanding,
that commands like a companion, orders like a friend,
harsh and tender as a comrade chieftain.
We see you each day a minister,
each day a soldier, each day
a simple person and difficult
each day.
And pure as a child
or as a man pure,
Che Comandante,
friend.

You pass in your discolored, torn,
hole-riddled campaign dress.
The one you wore in the jungle

fue el de la Sierra. Semidesnudo
el poderoso pecho de fusil y palabra,
de ardiente vendaval y lenta rosa.
No hay descanso.

      ¡Salud, Guevara!
O mejor todavía desde el hondón americano:
Espéranos. Partiremos contigo. Queremos
morir para vivir como tú has muerto,
para vivir como tú vives,
Che Comandante,
amigo.

octubre 15, 1967

as before you wore it in the Sierra.
Semi-naked
the mighty chest of the rifle and the word,
of blazing hurricane and lingering rose.
There can be no rest.

       Your health, Guevara!
Or better still, from the depths of America:
Wait for us. We will go with you. We want
to die to live as you have died,
to live as you live,
Che Comandante,
friend.

October 15, 1967

Ho Chi Minh

Al final del largo viaje,
Ho Chi Minh suave y despierto:
Sobre la albura del traje
le arde el corazón abierto.

No trae escolta ni paje.
Pasó montaña y desierto:
En la blancura del traje
sólo el corazón abierto.

No quiso más para el viaje.

Ho Chi Minh

After the long trip,
Ho Chi Minh gentle and awake:
an open heart burning
on the perfect whiteness of his gown.

He has no escort or valet.
He came over mountains and deserts:
with only an open heart
on the whiteness of his gown.

He wanted no more for the trip.

Note on Sources

The poems included in the second part of this anthology are taken from various sources, published and unpublished, as indicated below. The translations of the poems in the first part, as should be apparent, are the result of a collation and comparison of the versions appearing in the two editions of Guillén's *Antología mayor* (1964, 1969) and in the first and second editions of *El gran zoo* (1967, 1971).

Early Poems: 1920–1930
    The Future
    The Airplane
    The Clock
    The New Muse
    Rain
From *Sóngoro cosongo* (1931)
    The New Woman
    Madrigal
    Madrigal
    Sugarcane
From *West Indies, Ltd.* (1934)
    Riddles
    Sensemayá
    Madrigal ("Unadorned and vertical . . .")
    Guadeloupe, W.I.
    Sabás
From *Cantos para soldados y sones para turistas* (1937)
    Why, soldier, does it seem to you
    Soldiers in Abyssinia

WAYNESBURG COLLEGE LIBRARY
WAYNESBURG, PA.